WILDERNESS SURVIVAL ESSENTIALS

ROLF GUNDERSON

Copyright & Disclosures

TABLE OF CONTENTS

CHAPTER 1: INTRODUCTION

B asic instincts play a role in every single decision humans make, whether consciously or subconsciously. They are programmed into our internal makeup, almost as if on autopilot, to activate whenever we need them. All living things have two basic instincts in common: reproduction and survival. However, humans may address these two instincts differently than other living beings because of our ability to make maximum use of the resources available.

Surviving in the wilderness may not be something people think about every day, but it is the function of our survival instincts that would have us give the consideration its due. Popular television shows like AMC's The Walking Dead and CBS's Survivor entertain millions of people with story plots about surviving in unknown terrains and conditions, but watching them won't teach viewers about survival. To survive in the wilderness, you need to understand the essentials needed and know what to expect in a survival situation. You never know when one of these survival hacks may come in handy.

Let's take the Survival Rule of 3s, for instance. It is a great basic rule of thumb for outdoor survival that stipulates, on average, a human can live:

- 3 minutes without oxygen/air or immersed in icy water.
- 3 hours in harsh terrains without shelter (which includes clothing).
- 3 days without water, if they are sheltered from harsh terrains.
- 3 weeks without food, if they have shelter and water.

The great thing about the Rule of 3s is that it clarifies the maximum time frame humans can go without basic essentials in an easy-to-remember way. It also alerts us to what essentials we should prioritize in survival situations.

You'll know to pack plenty of food, a tent, appropriate clothing, and a couple of lighters and flint to prevent cold conditions and provide a heating source for cooking. Additionally, you're likely to bring your mobile phone along just in case an emergency arises that requires medical or official attention. But what happens if it rains? Or snows? Or even worse—you encounter an unexpected predator like a venomous spider, venomous snake, or hungry bear? That's where <u>Wilderness Survival Essentials</u> comes in handy.

This book will not only expound on the Survival Rule of 3s, but it will also walk you through the essentials needed to survive the most relevant wild terrain that you may find yourself subjected to. We'll cover:

- Survival essentials for extreme environments and conditions, like hypothermia and heatstroke.

- Preparing and building shelter, including sleeping bags, tents, camps, and natural shelters.

- Essential fire-making techniques, such as sparks, light/lens, friction, and chemical techniques to build your fire.

- The essentials of finding and storing a water supply, such as allowing birds to lead the way to water sources and preparing natural containers for storing water.

- Essential tools for surviving the wilderness, like flashlights, knives, saws, and spears.

- Survival essentials for your roping needs, including making natural cords by using resources like grass and plant fibers, knot basics, and hitching.

- Duress techniques for signaling for help with mirrors, flashlights, fire, and rocks.

- Finding food in the wilderness, including plants to avoid and baiting and catching techniques for fish and game.

Knowing the essentials to survive in the wilderness can be the difference between experiencing extreme panic when faced with elements in the wild versus being able to calmly and effectively handle whatever challenges come your way. The wilderness doesn't have to be a scary place that only the fittest are capable of surviving. This book will explain how anyone with a willingness to learn wilderness survival essentials can make it in the wild.

CHAPTER 2: EXTREME ENVIRONMENT

Most of us don't realize how unprepared we are to withstand extreme environments until we find ourselves in one. While it may not be too late to learn how to survive in an extreme environment once you are in this situation, being prepared ahead of time is recommended. Different extreme environments require different survival essentials. Campers will require different clothing and shelter than hikers, while canoers will require different resources than winter backpackers.

With millions of people visiting wilderness areas every year, half of which are within a day's drive of major cities, understanding how to survive these terrains is essential to hiker and backpacker safety. In this chapter, we'll cover some wilderness essentials for surviving in extreme conditions like rain, snow/ice, and heat/sun.

Rain

Rain is a factor all hikers and backpackers should prepare for. Many hikers and backpackers become the victims of an inaccurate weather forecast on a rainy day that was predicted to be warm and sunny. Whatever the case may be, it doesn't have to be a terrible day if you know some handy rainy weather survival essentials. When choosing your clothing for rainy conditions in the wilderness, consider the following:

Avoid cotton on your skin at all costs:

- Cotton absorbs moisture, including rain and even your own sweat.
- Cotton clothing on your skin chills you.
- Avoid cotton underwear (i.e. boxers, bras, etc.) as they can contribute to hypothermia.
- Choose clothing with wicking material instead (i.e. nylon, polyester, wool, etc.).

Don't forget the rain cap:

- Rain jackets with hoods, whether brimmed or not, just don't suffice in protecting your face or glasses from the rain.

- Ballcap-styled rain caps may be worn under the hood of your raincoat for added protection.

- Broad-brimmed rain caps are recommended.

Choose jackets that have synthetic insulation:

- Down jackets don't function as well when wet unless they are lined with synthetic insulation.

- For added protection, go with either water-resistant down jackets or down jackets with hybrid functionality that include both resistance to water and synthetic insulation.

- For milder weather, opt for soft-shell jackets or lightweight fleeces instead.

Evaluate your gear:

- Consider upgrading to rain gear in bright colors, as they can brighten your mood on rainy days and make it easier for emergency services to locate you.

Footwear:

- Waterproof footwear (i.e. shoes or boots) is great for keeping the water out initially but should be renewed at the start of each season or whenever large dark spots begin forming after encountering wet terrain.

- Mesh footwear offers faster drainage and drying after getting wet, making it a better option for milder conditions.

- Footwear with super traction is necessary when encountering slippery terrain (i.e. logs or rocks).

- Muddy terrains require footwear with deep lug soles.

Extras to pack for added protection:

- Don't forget to pack a few ziplock bags to make small possessions temporarily waterproof.

  — They don't take up much space and they're very light.

  — They are also handy for putting over socks before putting on boots to keep your socks and feet dry in rainy conditions.

- Include waterproof cases for your electronics (i.e. mobile phones, earphones, helmet cams, etc.).

- Line your gear pack with lightweight dry sacks to protect your most vulnerable belongings.

- Bring additional rain cover along with you, which may be included in your gear daypack or purchased separately to cover the size of your pack.

- Pack some trash bags as they provide multifunctional protection from the rain, including the ability to cover your gear pack or act as a tarp.

In addition to the above wet weather clothing and gear considerations, you can improve your ability to function in wet terrain with the following essentials:

Headlamp:

- It provides a hands-free light source as it attaches to headgear, allowing clear illumination of the terrain ahead.

Bandanas:

- Useful for drying off wet gear.

- Useful as a head covering as well.

- Multitowels may also be used, as they are synthetic as opposed to the cotton in bandanas.

Having the appropriate clothing, gear, and accessories to survive wet conditions prevents the rainy weather from ruining your trip. The key is keeping your skin dry and the water out of your clothing/pack.

Just knowing what to wear and bring isn't always enough—you will also need to know what to avoid and the best way to navigate.

Things to avoid in wet terrains include:

Flash floods, mudslides, and related hazards:

- Get familiar with your surroundings (i.e. locate danger and hazard signs that mark zones for floods, mudslides, or hazards).

- Avoid areas where flooding or mudslides are likely to occur.

- Don't hike in low areas like arroyos or along creek beds.

- Aim for high ground whenever possible.

Lightning:

- Avoid water (i.e. mud puddles, ponds, waterfalls, etc.) as lightning can still shock and kill you if it hits the water, even if the actual lightning doesn't strike you.

- Avoid camping or sheltering under trees or related areas in which lightning may strike unexpectedly.

- Refrain from using umbrellas or items with metallic materials that are likely to attract lightning.

- Avoid high ground areas when lightning is present as you may become the quickest path for the lightning to reach the ground.

- Choose areas lined with low-growing shrubs.

- If you need to retreat to a ditch or other depression for shelter, ensure no water is flowing into the area and stay as close to the ground as possible. Abandon the area if water begins flowing in.

- Wait at least thirty minutes after lightning or thunder has finished before leaving your safety zone.

Snow/Ice

Surviving snow or icy weather conditions may seem old-hat for anyone living in cold weather environments, but surviving cold conditions in the wilderness is vastly different from preparing for snowfall at your home. Even being exposed to cold weather in wild terrains for as few as five minutes can have devastating consequences because of the isolation.

Since snow and ice present wet conditions, many of the essentials described above for rainy weather may also be applied to extreme cold conditions. Along with rainy conditions, your main focus will be staying dry and warm; thus, the same water-resistance clothing and gear will be needed. However, you will also need to stay warm, so your clothing, gear, and accessories should be able to provide both functions. In addition, you'll want to have a separate winter essentials bug-out-bag (BOB), which is derived from the term 'bugging out' and refers to leaving your home for an unexpected emergency, etc.

A BOB serves as your survival kit stocked with essentials to help you survive an emergency, and your winter BOB is a prepacked bag with essentials needed to survive for at least 72 hours in extreme cold conditions in the wilderness.

Your winter BOB should be thick, durable, and water-resistant with airtight constriction. It should also be equipped with padded hip straps, additional pockets, and compartments for added storage. It may include a roll-top construction for even more expanded storage. When packing it, in addition to the wet weather essentials previously discussed, you should include:

1. Metal cups (for warming beverages and soups).
2. Cold weather clothing (sleeping bag for extra warmth).
3. Wool socks (for extra warmth - even if wet).
4. Long underwear (for extra warmth).
5. Hand and body warmers (for extra warmth).

6. Modern fire starters (i.e. flint, lighter/matches, magnesium, etc.).
7. Fire tinder such as paper towels or newspaper.
8. Ski goggles and ski mask (to protect your face).
9. Insulated water bottle (to keep beverages warm or hot for extended periods of time).
10. Reflector/space blankets (for attracting and absorbing heat).
11. Folding saw (for chopping wood, clearing pathways, and preparing shelter).

While your BOB and extreme cold weather essentials are helpful for surviving such conditions, staying warm and dry should be your number one priority. Not only are you at risk for frostbite, but you're also at risk for dangerous conditions like hypothermia. Thus, your priorities should be addressed as follows if staying for a long period of time (more than 4 hours):

1. Find or build a shelter (your BOB should be equipped with the resources to help).

   - If inside a vehicle (i.e. snowed in), remain inside your vehicle until help arrives.
   - If outside, seek caves or overhangs, create a makeshift snow cave by digging into a snowdrift, or construct a tent with the resources available to you.

2. Heat water to keep your body temperature up.

   - Cold water and eating snow results in an increase in calorie burn, which is counterproductive to your survival.

3. Start a fire to preserve your body temperature and maintain warmth.

4. Signal for help if you need to be rescued or require the aid of emergency responders (more on distress signaling in Chapter 7).

5. Find food if your BOB and/or other resources don't include enough food to last the duration of your trip.

- Build snare traps to hunt game.

In addition to the above, the following three are final reiterations for surviving in extreme cold conditions.

Prevent hypothermia by:

- Staying dry.
- Wearing the proper clothing and gear.
- Avoiding the wind.
- Keeping active.
- Building a fire.
- Consuming energy-rich food.

Treat frostbite as quickly as possible:

- Symptoms include numbness; tingly/cold fingers, toes, ears, or nose; stiff or waxy skin; and/or limited mobility of the joints.
- Mild frostbite may be treated by fifteen minutes of skin-to-skin contact to warm the body.
- Superficial frostbite may be treated by splinting and covering the impacted area of skin before loosening the clothing around it and seeking medical aid.
- Deep frostbite requires emergency attention (i.e. evacuation).

Heat/Sun

Extreme heat poses its own dangers, beyond the risks for sunburn, dehydration, hyponatremia, heat exhaustion, and heatstroke.

Sunburn is not only an annoying hazard, but it can also be significantly painful and uncomfortable. Although sunburn doesn't necessarily mean you're cooking your skin, it means that skin cells are under attack by ultraviolet radiation, which causes your skin to swell and redden hours after being exposed to the sun unprotected.

- Prevention is key—do your best to reduce sun exposure, keep your skin covered while in the sun, and use sunscreen.

Dehydration occurs when your body's water source is depleted from the loss of water (i.e. sweating).

- Mild depletion of water supply typically signals familiar symptoms, including dry mouth, increasing thirst levels, poignant urine that appears more yellow than usual, dizziness, headaches, and/or drowsiness.

- Severe water depletion results in quickened breathing, intense headaches and/or dizziness, increased pulse, dark yellow urine, feeling of confusion or lethargy, or even fainting.

- Monitor for signs of dehydration (i.e. urine frequency and color) in yourself and anyone you're with to stay ahead of severe dehydration.

  - A change in your usual urine frequency or failure to urinate every two or three hours is a good indicator of dehydration.

- Drink water more frequently until your urination frequency is back to normal, but be cautious not to overhydrate yourself with only plain water because doing so may lead to hyponatremia.

Hyponatremia occurs when profuse sweating from humidity and/or heat is combined with someone consuming only plain water for an extended time (i.e. days), causing your body's usual sodium supply to deplete to dangerously low levels.

- This may be deadly, especially for anyone already suffering from kidney problems or other related issues.
- Symptoms may be easily confused with dehydration.
- Mild symptoms include headaches, confusion, and drowsiness.
- Severe symptoms include mild to severe muscle cramps and spasms, confusion, and seizures.
- Electrolyte depletion without replacement can result in swelling of the brain, thereby leading to coma and/or death.
- To prevent it, you must steadily replace your salt and other electrolytes whenever you sweat profusely in extreme heat conditions.

  - Start by pouring a handful of sugar combined with a pinch of table salt into each gallon of water you drink.

  - Also, consider including oral rehydration salts (i.e. Drip Drop, NUUN) in your BOB or survival kit.

Heat exhaustion can be as deadly as hyponatremia and the combination of high temperatures and humid climates can be a recipe for disaster when you're out in the wilderness.

- Your body loses its ability to cool itself because the water-saturated air prevents the evaporation of perspiration.

- Symptoms may vary, including profuse sweating, clammy skin, extreme drowsiness, dizziness, and weakness.

- Your body's internal temperature will typically rise above 100° Fahrenheit—which happens to be the technical term for hyperthermia (not to be confused with hypothermia which is below the normal 98° Fahrenheit).

- Treat as soon as possible by seeking emergency services and taking the following steps:

    - Lay the victim down in the most shaded area available.
    - Slightly raise the victim's feet.
    - Have the victim drink plenty of cool liquid, preferably including electrolytes.
    - Proceed with the above until the victim recovers.
    - Allow the victim to rest for the remainder of the day and the day following the heat exhaustion to assure it doesn't reoccur.

Heatstroke (or severe hyperthermia) may occur if your body temperature reaches 104° Fahrenheit or above. Symptoms include dizziness, headache, hot dry skin, and loss of consciousness.

- Dry skin is the easiest symptom to identify, noticeable when a person stops perspiring.
- Request emergency services (i.e. 911) immediately.
- Move the victim to the coolest place available.
- Raise the victim's head and cool their body with a wet cloth or article of clothing while also fanning them to help lower their body temperature.
- Monitor the victim's temperature to see when it goes below 104° Fahrenheit, then replace the victim's wet clothing with dry clothing as you resume monitoring.
- Monitor for any signs of shock and be prepared to offer resuscitative services if warranted.
- Get the victim to a medical facility or professional as soon as possible.

Chapter Summary

Knowing how to survive extreme conditions can be the difference between life and death during hazardous circumstances. Having the proper clothing and gear enhances your ability to weather these conditions, but remaining calm and knowing what to do to prevent and handle these dangerous conditions are key to your survival.

Understanding the risks that different types of extreme environments pose will help you address your survival in these conditions. Now you should have the groundwork for surviving just about any extreme environment you may find yourself in while exploring the wilderness.

In this chapter, you learned:

- The hazards that extreme weather conditions pose when in the wilderness.
- Survival essentials for surviving extreme rain/wet conditions in the wilderness.
- Survival essentials for surviving extreme cold conditions in the wilderness.
- Survival essentials for surviving extreme heat conditions in the wilderness.

In the next chapter, you will learn about finding and building shelter to survive in the wilderness.

CHAPTER 3: SHELTER

Finding or building shelter in the wilderness is just as crucial as preparing yourself for the elements as it will also protect you against animals and insects. As briefly discussed in the previous chapter, survival shelters can range from tents and sleeping bags to manmade shelters using natural or available resources.

As the Rule of 3s prescribes, you can only survive for up three hours in extreme conditions without shelter. Therefore, the three-hour window of survival should be highly focused on locating or building shelter. Locating shelter may be as simple as retreating to your RV or Winnebago, locating a cave, or spotting an abandoned shack. Building shelter, on the other hand, will depend on what is packed in your BOB or other travel packs/gear, along with the natural resources available to you.

Locate coverage:

- Your natural surroundings (i.e. large trees and protruding rocks/stones/walls) can offer invaluable protection if you're unable to build or find other readily available forms of shelter.

Provide elevation for your bedding:

- Elevating your bed helps keep you dry and enhances your protection from insects and other creepy crawlers.

- Insulate your bedding from the ground with twigs, etc.—similar to a bird's nest.

Stay dry at all costs:

- As thoroughly advised in Chapter 1, staying dry is crucial to your survival in the wilderness.

- It's much more difficult to dry yourself in the wilderness and get your body warmed back to safe core temperatures than it is to stay dry and prevent any exposure to wet conditions.

- Preparation is key.

Prepackaged Shelter

When locating shelter is not a viable option, you'll need to use the resources at your immediate disposal, and your travel pack and BOB are great places to start. In addition to the essentials previously discussed, you'll want to consider including ultralight shelters like tents, tarps, sleeping bags, and ground pads in your packs or BOBs. A shelter is considered to be an ultralight shelter when it lacks poles dedicated to maintaining its structure, so some self-standing tents are not considered ultralight shelters. Whether poled or ultralight, prepackaged shelter is always a good resource to include in your travel pack or BOB. Often, when wilderness travelers find themselves in need of shelter, they are already low on energy, making it that much more difficult to build a shelter with natural resources. Thus, you should consider traveling with the following prepackaged shelter options:

Tents. There are many tents available for various camping needs. Although tents can be costly and are typically heavier and less versatile than some other shelters, they do offer considerable benefits. Some pros of packing a tent into your travel pack or BOB include:

- Relatively easy setup.
- Self-standing once they have been set up.

- Provides shield from water and protection from weather and insects.

Tarps.

Tarps are cheaper, lighter, and more versatile than tents, but they aren't self-standing or as weatherproof, and don't provide protection from insects. However, they offer more flexibility than tents and allow you to build a variety of shelter shapes. They also allow for fresh air circulation and can make you feel closer to nature. For instance, a lean-to allows you to prepare dinner while protected from the wind but still being able to view the night sky. Typically, tarp shelters are used for the following scenarios:

- **Ultralight Shelters** - When tarps are used instead of tents for lighter weight packing.

- **Section Options/Plan Bs** - When a tarp is packed as the last resort in the event you're unable to reach a physical shelter.

- **Hammocks** - People who prefer to sleep in hammocks while outdoors may opt to pitch a tarp above the hammock for overhead protection.

- **Survival** - Survivalists often like carrying tarps, just in case they find themselves in conditions in which it's the best sheltering option.

Sleeping Bags.

A sleeping bag is another important essential for your sheltering needs, and you will benefit from its use in just about any outdoor wilderness environment. The key is packing the appropriate sleeping bag for your journey. When making your selection, the following characteristics should be taken into consideration:

<u>Shape</u>:

- **Rectangular sleeping bags** maximize roominess but aren't as warm as mummy bags.

- **Semi-rectangular sleeping bags,** aka barrel-shaped or modified-mummy bags, come in various shapes for comfort, but some designs tend to compromise either warmth or roominess.

- **Mummy bags** are slim and hooded to provide more warmth and less weight, offering a snug fit.

<u>Temperature Rating</u>:

- Consider the climate in which the sleeping bag will be used by researching the historical temperatures in the area:

- Identify the average low temperature for the winter months in the area you will be using your sleeping bag in. Use that number to select a sleeping bag with an appropriate comfort rating to accommodate the climate you'll be in.

- Select a sleeping bag with an EN comfort rating equal to or colder than your expected average low for the climate the bag will be used in.

Insulation:

Down Insulation: Generally considered to be more expensive, but also lighter in weight and offers more compression for easier packing.

- Retains warmth for more years than synthetic insulation.
- Usually treated with water-resistant material.
- Durable.
- Performs well in cold, dry conditions.

Synthetic Insulation: Typically cheaper than down insulation and durable even when wet.

- Insulates even when wet.
- Dries fast.
- Hypoallergenic.
- Ideal for damp climates.

Ground Pads.

Many people pack a ground pad as an extra layer of protection from the ground in your tent, tarp, or sleeping bag. Alternatively, if you bring a sleeping bag, it may have a ground or sleeping pad included (the temperature rating displayed on your bag is based on testing with a sleeping pad; R-value, so sleeping pads with higher R-values offer more insulation. The higher the better).

CHAPTER 4: NATURAL SHELTER

N atural Shelter

While a prepackaged shelter is ideal, it's more likely that anyone requiring wilderness survival essentials will not have a prepackaged shelter with them. Therefore, they will have to rely on whatever resources they have available and bend them to their needs. Natural resources are likely to be available and the rest of this book will be primarily focused on non-prepackaged wilderness essentials, beginning with natural shelters. Natural shelters are considered any natural resource that can shield you from the elements (rain, cold, heat, wind, etc.).

Reserving your energy is a crucial priority when trying to survive in the wilderness. Being able to find natural shelter goes a long way in preserving your energy, especially if you can find a shelter that requires no work on your part, such as a cave or a natural windbreak. Use caution when considering natural shelters as they may already be inhabited. This can include during the day as well as partial natural night-time habitation for venomous and predatory animals. If you can locate one of the following natural shelters, you will be able to conserve the energy you would use building a shelter:**Caves**: Arguably the best type of natural resource available when locatable:

- **Dual Purpose**: Protects against the elements and shields you from potential dangers/prey.

- Use caution when entering because it may already be inhabited (i.e. others seeking shelter, animals, bats, wild game, etc.).

- Set up camp near the entrance just in case you find an imminent need to vacate.

- Be wary of starting a fire near the rock wall because the heat build-up can encourage cracks and cause rocks to fall, posing a considerable risk. Build reflector fires instead that you can lay near for warmth.

- Don't build a fire that will block the entrance and keep it small so it doesn't use all the oxygen in the cave.

Rock Formations: They take many shapes and forms, so finding the perfect formation for shelter without any additional work on your part can be challenging.

Abandoned Structures: Surprisingly more common than most people think:

- There's a good chance that the wilderness area you're trying to withstand has been previously inhabited by people at some point in history.

- Even when they don't provide full shelters, they are a great base to build a shelter and offer at least a wind-break.

Deadfalls: Fallen trees often offer great shelter through the exposed roots from the trunk that is lying on the ground:

- A tarp can be pitched over the trunk for added shelter.

- The root exposure of the trunk can serve as the basis of a lean-to shelter (discussed further in the following section).

Undercut Banks: Not suitable in situations involving heavy rain; otherwise, a great singular-sided form of shelter:

- Great for pitching tarps.

Animal Dens: Caution needed because some may still be inhabited by animals. Dens may likely require work to enlarge them for sheltering:

- Sizes vary based on inhabitants (i.e. dug out holes, cleared brush, etc.).

Trees: Provide a variety of sheltering options:

- **Pine trees** have long branches that often extend near or to the ground, making them ideal instant shelters.

- **Large shade trees** are great for shielding you from rain.

- **Hollow trees** are more likely to be found in forests with towering trees.

- Great for immediate shelter when available.

Since locating fully constructed natural shelters is not always possible, wilderness survivalists often have to build on what is available. As noted above, trees are a great natural resource to use as a base for building your shelter. However, just as with caves and other natural habitats, there are animals and bugs to be on the lookout for when picking trees for shelter. For instance, though small and seemingly nonthreatening, ants often inhabit trees and can become a nuisance when you disturb their habitat. There also may be wild game occupying the tree or surrounding trees. Just watch the tree and surrounding trees for potential problems before building your shelter.

Tree shelters can be built from the ground up (i.e. deadfalls) or built above off-the-ground structures. We'll cover sheltering options for both tree-type shelters and you can pick which one is best, based on your circumstances:

#On-Ground Shelters:

1. Lean-to

One of the more common forms of shelters used, as it can be set up easily and provides great wind protection:

Overhung or **fallen trees** serve as a wall for you to pitch your lean-to shelter, but you can also build a wall if unable to locate an overhung or fallen tree.

- The wall is your foundation and must be sturdy enough to withstand the total weight of your roofing materials.

- If you're unable to find an overhung or fallen tree, look for a log or long stick that can be propped up as support for your roof:

- Use a tree limb or two sticks to prop up each side of the log/long stick, creating an overhead horizontal structure to support the weight of your roofing material.

- Collect more sticks and/or branches for your lean-to structure and arrange them closely on the horizontal structure at a 45° angle, minimizing openings for any wind, water or debris to seep through.

- For wet weather, if your wall is facing the rain, consider making the angle deeper (60° angle) to prevent leaking into your shelter.

- Collect any available debris you can find to construct your lean-to wall, including bark, leaves, boughs, pine needles, and twigs. However, use caution as animals like snakes may be lurking underneath dry debris.

- Assemble the debris thickly to plug up gaps between the sticks.

- Stack a few small branches on top to hold things in place.

- You can also consider adding ribs on the side of your newly constructed shelter for extra protection from the wind.

2. Debris Shelters

This is a harder shelter to build, even considered the last resort option to some, but provides insulation to keep you warm without a fire.

- You'll need to construct a ridgepole by using the crook of a tree, a strong stick, or two sticks bound together with a cord or twine.

- Collect branches that may be structured as two uprights to support the ridgepole if needed and tie them together on each side to prop up the ridgepole.

- Place the ridgepole in the grooves of the upright to form your roof, then secure it with the cord or twine.

- Secure the other end of the ridgepole on the ground. A heavy rock is sometimes used to keep the other end in place.

- Add sticks on each side to create the walls of the shelter.

- Add ribs to the side with smaller sticks, but don't arrange them above the ridgepole because it may cause water to leak inside or cause the ridgepole to break altogether.

- Gather debris, such as dead leaves, pine needles, and/or dead grass to use to form a thick bed (at least one to two feet), the walls, and for the floor of your shelter. It will insulate you from the ground, shield you from the air, and serve as your resting place.

- A door may be added for extra warmth by collecting branches to tie together at the entrance if desired.

3. Fallen Trees

Root balls and tree trunks from fallen trees offer great sheltering opportunities:

- Root balls often provide sufficient roofing or walling for shelter. Tarps may be used for additional overhead coverage or for ground padding to protect against direct ground contact or insects.

- Root balls from trees that have fallen long before your arrival may be more flexible and allow for bending and clearing for expanded shelter.

- Tree trunks can be great resources for walls, roofing, or ridgepoles, and can also be a base for pitching tarp for more walling or roofing.

4. Teepees (Tipi)/Wicki-up Shelters

One of the oldest forms of manmade shelters available, these shelters are designed to fit two to three people, they allow for starting a fire inside without posing a risk, and may also be used for long-term use.

- Conical (cone-like) structure.

- Collect three 7-8 feet long, thick logs (at least 6-8 inches thick) for your tripod base:

- Fasten the top of the three logs together with a cord or twine, then spread out the three ends in a conical shape.

- Secure the bottoms of the three logs into the ground with stones or by sharpening the bottom of each log to dig into the ground for security.

- Collect more logs to fill in between the three large conical-shaped logs (fill until there are no gaps) and make sure they are secure.

- Stack debris onto the outside of the structure from the bottom up until completely covered.

- Create a bed inside by stacking thick leaves or soft debris.

5. Round Lodge Shelters

Similar to teepees/wicki-ups, but these include a solid doorway and are typically constructed with a hole in the roof or a sunroof:

- Sunroof allows for building fires without posing a risk.

- May be built with thatched grass or thick debris.

Off-Ground Tree Shelters:

1.Nests

Just like birds, you can build a large nest above the ground in a tree using wood, rocks, and debris:

- Use debris like vegetation, tall grass, and evergreen and fern boughs for the first layer that will surround you in the nest.

- Build a sloping roof using wood (i.e. tree branches/sticks).

2. Bough Bed

Provides an elevated shelter with relative ease:

- Collect two 7-8 feet long, thick logs (at least 6 inches) and two 4-5 feet long logs:

- Place the long logs on the ground next to each other.

- Lay the two shorter logs across the long logs.

- Fasten the logs together with twine or a cord to secure them.

- Collect small sticks to stack on top of the long logs for the frame of your bed, then tie them together with twine or a cord.

- Collect soft needles, pine, spruce, dry leaves, or debris to pile together for the bedding cushion.

3.Bog Ken/Platform Shelter

Built on stilts with various designs, but a common lean-to platform design may be built as follows:

- Gather two 8-9 feet long logs.

- Dig two 6-inch holes into the ground to drive each log into firmly, then fill the holes with mud for added security.

- Repeat the above steps with two slightly smaller logs, placing them parallel to the larger poles. This will create a 2x1 meter rectangle-shape frame.

- Gather two more thick logs to assemble on top to connect the other four with and form your thatched roof, which should be at a 30° angle once assembled.

- Add ribs to the side for extra security.

- Stack debris on top of the roof from the bottom up and secure with rocks or branches to protect against the wind.

- Collect two more logs for the platform, placing them in the form of a crossbar, then secure them by tying them to the lower end of the roof and tying them in a straight line to the long log.

- Collect grass and broad leaves to stack together on top of the frame to form your bed, ensuring the length of the bed is the same length as the shelter, so it can be properly placed on the crossbars.

Tarp Shelters

For travelers with tarps, the following sheltering options are also viable:

1. Wedge/C-Fly Tarp Shelter

Great option for areas experiencing windy conditions, as it's designed with an aerodynamic shape that facilitates its ability to resist strong winds and heavy rain:

- Lay your tarp onto the ground between two trees.

- Use 2-4 pegs to secure a tarp into the ground at the long side edge.

- Form an edge line between the trees, then fold the remainder of the tarp, covering over that edge line.

- Use more pegs to secure the edges of the overlaying roof into the ground.

2. Elevated horizontal roof

Also provides good protection from wind and rain:

- Use pegs to secure the rear-middle section of the tarp to the ground (this is the back of your shelter).

- Tie a long, sturdy stick at the front of the tarp to elevate the entrance.

- Secure the edges of the front two corners into the ground with pegs.

- Secure the edges of the back two corners into the ground with pegs.

- You can make adjustments for additional headroom by resizing and repositioning the pole, elevating the entrance.

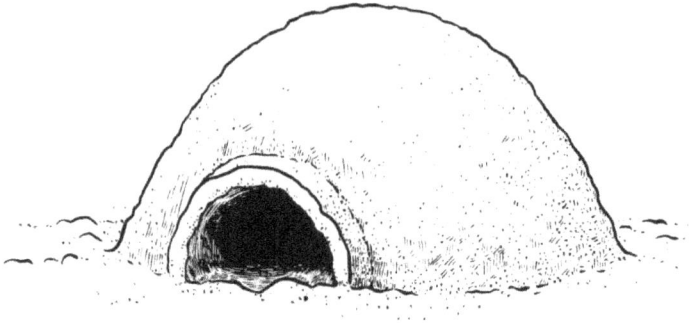

Snow Cave/Quinzee Shelters:

Often the only option for survivalists located in deep snow areas, this is arguably one of the most dangerous types of shelters to build when the snow selection isn't adequately checked-out. A Quinzee is made by piling the snow in the form of a dome and then hollowing out the shelter from the inside.

To build a Quinzee shelter, you should:

- Pile your equipment or some easily removable pine branches in the form of a dome, etc. in the desired location.

- Cover the pile with a tarp if you have one.

- Bury your pile with snow in the shape of a dome about 7 feet high. Pack the snow covering to at least a depth of 2 feet of snow on top of your equipment pile or 7 feet total (more snow if you don't have a large pile).

- Wait about 2 hours for the snow covering to compact and freeze together. This is often called "sintering".

- While waiting for the sintering, break some sticks into 1 foot to 1.5-foot lengths. Stick these into the snow toward your equipment pile while it is sintering. These sticks will be used to measure the walls to be 1 to 1.5 feet thick.

- After 2 hours, dig an entrance that isn't facing the wind and start pulling out your equipment and stuffing materials. This will leave a hollowed-out area.

- Climb into the hollow where your supplies/stuffing used to be and begin gently scraping the snow until you hit a stick. You know the wall is about 1 to 1.5 feet thick now.

- For ventilation, dig a 6-inch hole into the roof.

Precautions

- It doesn't always provide enough oxygen to sustain habitation. Make sure to add a ventilation hole.

- The ceiling runs the risk of collapse, which can result in the inhabitants getting buried alive. However, the walls aren't that thick so you should be able to stand up and be OK.

Setting Up Camp

You should also prioritize finding a suitable location to set up camp. If the camp location isn't chosen wisely, you could be uncomfortable or exposed to unnecessary danger. You'll want to focus on safe areas that also offer the necessary resources such as wood and water.

When choosing your location, you should consider the following five vital factors:

1.Water.

Areas with water are good to camp near because you can have a nearby source of water. However, you don't want to set up camp too close to the water because it may end up posing a risk to your shelter.

- Take note of high and low terrain and look for signs of erosion (i.e. dirt or leaves that seem unnaturally settled in a specific direction).

- Set up camp at least 200-300 yards away from the water source to ensure you're close enough for quick access while also being far enough away so the water won't pose any threat to predators or sudden changes in water flow (flash floods).

- Avoid setting up camp in low areas where water may pool if a rainstorm occurs.

2.Wind.

Wind not only affects your sheltering options, but it can also drop your body's core temperature.

- When choosing areas to set up camp, notice the wind direction because your shelter will need to block the wind.

- A light breeze will help keep the mosquitoes and other bugs away.

- If you encounter areas with varying wind directions, it may be best to opt for a different location that doesn't have multi-directional winds.

- Camping in areas with natural elements like heavy vegetation or rock outcrops will help with blocking unwanted wind from your campsite.

- Be mindful that night air flows downhill as it cools and settles in valleys so camping higher is normally better.

3. Sun.

Warming up to the rising sun.

- Choose a place where the rising sun will warm you up.

- The rising sun will help dry out your shelter and clothes in the morning.

4.Wood.

Wood will be your primary source of fire, so you want to choose a location that has a sufficient supply of wood suitable for building and sustaining a fire.

- Wood for starting your fire will need to be small in size (i.e. roughly between 2-6 inches long) because it will dry and burn faster and will allow the fire to build the heat needed to grow.

- Keep the fire burning with larger pieces of wood (i.e. at least the size of your wrist), so locating dead fallen trees may provide a good resource for wood to sustain your fire.

- In wet conditions, deadfall (wood on the ground) will be wet so look for dead, low-hanging branches on trees to break off. They're typically drier because they're protected by the branches above and they dry faster because they're exposed to the wind.

5. Wildlife. Being aware of the wildlife in the area you're camping in can save you from encountering unwanted danger.

- Be aware of wild game in the area you're traveling to before traveling there whenever possible.

- Scout the area for signs of wildlife (i.e. tracks, game trails, or scat) before setting up your campsite.

- Avoid camping too close to a game trail.

6. Widowmakers. Rotting/rotted trees can result in fatal deadfalls, so you want to be sure your campsite doesn't pose the risk of falling rocks or branches, especially since this will be your sleeping area and you want to prevent encountering any danger while rebuilding your energy.

- Observe both overhead and underneath the area for any potential dangers or signs of danger (i.e. visual signs of decay found at the base of tree trunks).

- Watch rock overhangs for rocks that may dislodge in a rainstorm, etc.

- With trees of various heights, the direction of a deadfall can be unpredictable, so it is crucial to ensure there are no visible signs of decay, even for trees that appear healthy.

- Be aware that tree branches for tall trees appear much smaller than they actually are when viewing them from the ground. You don't want to realize their actual size by having them crash down on your campsite.

Building a Fire Pit

While fire building techniques will be discussed in more detail in the next chapter, it is an important consideration when choosing your camp location. When choosing a location suitable for a fire pit, you want to be able to redirect the heat toward yourself and prevent a runaway fire.

- A circular wall of rocks helps keep the fire contained.

- Make sure your fire pit is at least 10 feet away from your shelter if it's a natural shelter because these shelters pose a greater risk of going up in flames if ignited by a tiny spark from the fire pit.

- Tents and tarps can easily be burned from sparks/cinders from the fire pit, so be aware of the direction that the wind will blow them.

- Locations with bushes, rocks, and fallen trees are great for blocking the wind from affecting your fire.

- Many campers opt to build their fire pits to the east of their shelter because westward blowing wind is most common across most of the west coast of the United States.

- Gather wood to keep near your campsite to fuel your fire. Keep the wood 10 feet away from the fire to prevent accidental fires from sparks.

- For extra installation from the ground, stack up pine boughs or other nearby soft debris and build the fire on top. This is handy for building a fire on wet ground.

Food and Bathroom

Two final considerations that should be made when deciding where to set up camp are food and bathroom.

Food

Your safety is important so you want to avoid attracting potential predators. Food is a major attraction for predatory game. To safeguard your food and yourself from encountering predators attracted by food, avoid leaving any traces of food at your campsite (i.e. crumbs, scraps of eaten food). It is also a good idea to store your food away from your campsite in a nearby location such as a tree.

Bathroom

Don't pee into a body of water because this contaminates the water. It is better to pee at least 100 feet from water and on a rock where it will evaporate quickly. Don't pee into the wind or uphill.

Not only does the food you prepare attract predators, but your bathroom activity can also draw unwanted wild game. Feces can attract animals to your campsite and contaminate your water supply. Bury your poop by digging a hole 6-8 inches deep to dump it in along with any toilet paper and then cover the hole with dirt and debris.

Going to the bathroom will also result in a need to cleanse yourself afterward. In the unfortunate event that you don't have a preferred method of cleaning up available to you (i.e. tissue, cloth, etc.), resist the urge to reach for fresh leaves on living trees if you can. While they may seem like your best option because they are soft and flexible, it may be a poisonous plant. Instead, choose moss, leaves, or grasses that you know are not poisonous. However, a smooth, clean rock is actually a better and safer option.

Chapter Summary

Surviving in the wilderness requires serious consideration, on-the-spot planning, and effective execution. While being prepared with a travel pack or BOB is optimal, there is always the chance you won't have either when you find yourself needing (not simply desiring) to survive the outdoors. Knowing where and how to build a shelter will be crucial to your survival. The options presented to you in this chapter will go a long way in preparing you to survive the unexpected should you find yourself needing to set up camp and build a shelter in the wilderness.

In this chapter, you learned:

- How to prepare prepackaged shelters in the wilderness.
- How to build natural shelters in the wilderness.
- How to build tarp shelters in the wilderness.
- How to build snow caves/igloos in the wilderness.
- Necessary considerations for choosing your location to set up your campsite in the wilderness.
- Necessary considerations for storing food and using the bathroom in the wilderness.

In the next chapter, you will learn various techniques for building a fire.

CHAPTER 5: FIRE

B eing able to build a fire is critical to your survival in the wilderness if you are going to be there for more than a day. Fire provides the necessary heat to keep you warm, and also functions as a heating source to warm liquids (needed to sustain your internal body temperature) and cook food. Luckily, there are many ways to build a fire, which include using natural elements along with manmade resources.

No matter what method is used to build your fire, three essential elements remain necessary for creating any type of fire: **air, fuel, and heat**:

Air provides the oxidation needed to sustain a fire:

- Air generally contains about 21% of oxygen.

- Fire generally requires about 16% of oxygen to facilitate burning.

- The chemical process that results from igniting a fire is supported by the oxygen in the surrounding area, as the fire continuously reacts by releasing heat and producing combustion by way of smoke, embers, and gases.

Fuel may be typically associated with gas or oil, but it actually includes any type of combustible material. Fuel is generally characterized based on its size, shape, quantity, and its moisture content (which affects its ability to burn).

Heat (or a heat source) is needed to ignite the initial fire and to start, sustain, and keep your fire from spreading. Heat dries out and preheats surrounding fuel sources which is why a fire pit/circle is needed to contain the fire.

Understanding these three key elements to build a fire will help you better understand the process of building and sustaining your fire.

Sparks

Building a fire by using sparks is probably the easiest way to build a fire, but that measure of ease can vary based on the source used to ignite the spark. The spark method requires something that is easy to ignite such as tinder or cloth. Tinder may be the easiest resource to use in the wilderness because it can be anything from dry leaves or grass to bark and dry pine needles, to twigs and wood shavings. Thus, nearby debris can become tinder for your fire when available. Note that whatever source is used to ignite the spark must be dry. This is because water suffocates a fire and air is needed for a fire.

Char Cloth: A useful form of tinder is a char cloth, but it has to be created, which is done by burning cotton cloth in a low-oxygen environment. This results in a black charcoal that makes it easy for a spark to grow into a fire.

- Place 1 or 2 pieces of cotton from a T-shirt or denim jeans into an Altoid Mint tin.

- Use a small nail to put a hole in the tin. This must be a very small hole.

- Bury the tin in the coals of a fire for 15 to 20 minutes.

- Remove from the coals and let cool. Gently remove the char cloth because it will tend to disintegrate in your fingers.

- Catch a spark on the char cloth to create an ember. Gently blow on the ember to grow it. As the ember grows, it will reach a point where it will burst into flames.

Lighters are the simplest method to use for igniting your spark, so if you have a lighter with you, building your fire will be much easier. Ignite the tinder or cloth to get the fire started, then you can build on it with gradually larger sticks and wood.

The **Flint and Steel** combination is considered the most reliable spark method because it is an almost unlimited source of sparks.

- Flint is a form of quartz, which is an extremely hard rock.
- Striking 2 pieces of flint together generates a spark.
- Striking flint against steel also creates a spark.
- Keep your wrist-movement as loose as possible when striking the flint and steel.
- It's easiest to use the char cloth to start the fire but any tinder can be used.
- Create a small bundle of tinder from grasses or tree bark. Including some dry pine needles is also helpful because pine needles are very combustible.
- Continue striking the flint and steel until a spark lands in your tinder to create an ember. Then gently blow on it to spread the ember and create a flame for starting the fire.

Firesteel magnesium is another great source for sparking a fire when available. To spark your fire with this method, you'll need tinder or another flammable source, a scraper (i.e. knife or flint), and firesteel or a magnesium stick:

- Place your scraper or the scraping edge of your knife against the firesteel or magnesium stick at a 30° or 45°-angle and scrape down with adequate pressure to ignite a spark on your timber.

- Only strike down to about half a centimeter from the bottom of the firesteel or magnesium stick to avoid extinguishing the flames before they get going.

- As above, catch the spark on a char cloth or tinder and then gently blow on the growing ember until a flame appears.

Light/Lens

To start a fire in the wilderness on a sunny day, you can use the light and lens method. You'll need a convex lens to concentrate the light on the tinder. Convex lenses are thicker in the middle than on the edges and can be found in eyeglasses, magnifying glasses, flashlights, camera lenses, binocular lenses, or telescopic lights. You can also focus light with a silver parabolic mirror, or even a polished soda can. This method offers an indefinite number of fire-starting opportunities, as long as you have plenty of sun and tinder to start your fire and wood to keep it burning.

Follow these steps to create a fire with a lens and light:

- Angle the lens so that the sunlight is focused on your pile of tinder. Move the lens closer and farther from the tinder until you find the spot of maximum light concentration where the light is brightest and also smallest.

- Keep the lens held over the same spot until the concentrated light causes the tinder to begin smoldering.

- Gently fan or blow the tinder to further oxidize it into a flame and build up your fire, then place it over your pit.

If you don't have a readily available lens to concentrate your light with, you can use natural resources like ice or water to create a lens.

Lens from Ice

When using ice, the objective is to use sources that don't contain gas bubbles, so try to locate ice from a pond or clear lake to use for your lens. To shape the ice into a lens, scrape it into form with a knife or grind it with a rock or stone. Make sure the middle is thicker than the edges (a convex lens). Then, smooth it out by using the heat from your hands as a heating source. Keep in mind that larger lenses are better because they can collect more light, so try to aim for a lens around 2 inches thick and at least 7 inches in diameter.

Once your lens is formed, hold it over your tinder at an angle perpendicular to the sun, then focus the brightest beam of light onto your tinder until it smokes and ignites. Make sure no water drips from your ice lens onto your tinder, so it remains dry for ignition.

Lens from Water

Another alternative, if you don't have a ready-made lens available to concentrate the light with, is a **water bottle/container**. You'll need to fill the bottle or container with water, but you have to make sure there are no air bubbles. Next, flip the bottle or container upside down so you can see the rounded bottom to use as your lens for concentrating the light onto your tinder (paper with dark ink works best as tinder for this method, so if you have it handy, use it instead of debris).

A few other options for starting a fire with light and a non-traditional lens include:

- **Coke Can**—A coke can or a can with a similar metallic bottom can be used to concentrate the light, but you'll need to polish the bottom of the can (a chocolate bar is a great resource for polishing if you happen to have one) to make it shiny.

- **Flashlight**—Without damaging the rest of the flashlight, remove the glass from the cover and take out the silver cup, which should be shaped like a cone or funnel. Fill the bottom, narrow portion of the silver cup with tinder, then angle the silver cup toward the light to concentrate it and ignite the tinder.

- **Plastic Wrap**—Same as the water bottle method, except the plastic wrap serves as a magnifying glass.

- **Empty Light Bulb**—Same as the water bottle method, except the empty light bulb serves as a magnifying glass.

Friction

Starting a fire by friction is a more tiring process than the prior two methods discussed. It requires patience and technique, which makes it one of the more temperamental fire-starting techniques as well. Although it may not be the technique most rush to deploy to get their fires started, the concept behind friction fires is easily understandable as we commonly do it in our everyday lives.

One instance that you have likely used friction to develop heat is when your hands are cold and you rub them together. Rubbing causes the molecules that touch to move faster which generates energy. More energy means more heat. For another example to illuminate how much heat friction can generate, consider your childhood days speeding down a slide with your hands clenching the sides for dear life and the sting from the burn that the friction generated. That's the power of natural energy, which becomes a major asset when short on resources to start your fire while stuck in the wilderness.

To apply the theory of friction to the three essentials for starting a fire (air, fuel, and heat), friction becomes your source of heat. Your environment will provide the air and the objects used to generate the friction, which will erode when rubbing them at the source of fuel. The key is choosing the correct objects with which to generate the friction since they must be able to generate heat and erode into a source for fuel. Two common methods for starting friction fires are **hand drill** and **bow drill**.

Hand Drill.

The hand drill method is one of the simpler methods for spinning to generate friction. It requires the use of a long, thin spindle, a hearth board, and your hands. Generating friction by way of spinning is an effective method because the energy generated is concentrated on one spot. Although considered one of the simplest methods, don't confuse simplicity with ease of execution—it is one of the most difficult spinning methods to execute because it relies solely on your hands and strength. If you are patient and methodical with your execution, you can reduce the mental frustration that's often associated with this difficult task.

Selecting the proper materials is key.

- The drill or spindle should be a long, straight stick (i.e. between 1-2 feet) of dead and dry wood (wood that is green or has moisture will not work to generate the friction needed to yield heat). The drill may be sanded or scraped with a rock to smooth it out since your palms will be spinning it. The thicker end of the drill is usually used for friction and rubbed against the board.

- The hearth board should be as flat as possible, at least twice as wide as the drill you'll be using and about half an inch thick. The bottom half of the board should be flat enough to prevent wobbling (basswood, cedar wood, and weeping willow wood are good options for a board). You'll need to punch out a pilot hole in the board (roughly ⅛ inch deep) as a slot for the drill to sit in. You can use a sharp rock to form this but be sure to position the hole at least a ½ inch from the edge of the board.

- Notch the edge of the board by carving at a 45°-angle.

- Place your knee or foot on the board to hold it in place, then begin spinning the drill between your hands into the pilot hole while pressing down with considerable pressure to create the hole.

- Place some dead leaves or pieces of bark underneath the board to shield it from the moisture of the ground before you start drilling. You'll also want to place dry material (i.e. a chip of wood or a thick dry leaf) under the notch you created, so the sawdust created through your drilling may be collected.

- Sit or kneel near the drill with a knee or foot on the board to hold it in place. Moisten your hands with spit or dried-up pine before you begin drilling so you're better able to grip the drill.

- Spin the drill as fast as possible while applying pressure down onto the board in a continuous motion to generate heat and fuel. As your hands slide down the drill, you'll want to hold the drill in place in the hole with one hand while quickly moving your way back up to the top of the drill. You should do this to get back to spinning as fast as possible and preserve the heat you're generating.

- Continue drilling until smoke appears and your notch is full of sawdust. Once your notch is full of dust and continuously spewing out dark brown dust, speed up your drilling for several runs to ignite the dust. You want the dust to glow or generate several seconds worth of smoke to ensure an ember/coal has formed.

- Once the ember has formed, carefully carry the board over to your pile of tinder and nest the ember in the tinder before enclosing it in a bundle. Then, blow gently to fan the ember into a flame.

Bow Drill.

The bow drill is the most widely recognized friction fire-starting method known in the northern hemisphere. It's also one of the friction fire-starting methods people choose to experiment with first because it can be used on a bigger variety of wood than other methods. Similar to the hand drill, you'll need a spindle and hearth board for this technique, and you can apply the same techniques needed for hand drilling to the specifications of your drill and board for the bow drill method. However, instead of using your hands, you'll need a bow.

- Your bow should be made with wood that is flexible enough to spring and maintain tension against rope (willow limbs are a good option).

- Find a piece of wood that fits comfortably in your hand and carve a hole into the end of it. This will be the top handhold for your bow drill.

- For your bow, find a slightly curved stick around the length of your arm and with a base that's about as thick as your thumb. Tie a string or vine to the bottom of the stick, then bend it to tie the other end of string or vine to the top of the stick, ensuring that the knot is easily adjustable. Leave enough slack in the string or vine to allow room for your spindle to be twisted in, but not so much slack that it's at risk of slipping around.

- Drill holes into your hearth board and handhold with a knife or sharp rock to prevent the spindle from slipping out while drilling.

- Secure the hearth board with your left knee or foot to the left of the notch carved into it. Position your other knee comfortably behind your left foot in a kneeling position.

- Twist the spindle into the hearth board as follows:

- Secure the thick end of the bow under your right arm and against your side, freeing up your hands. The string should be over the bow.

- Position the rounded end of your spindle on the right of the hearth board with the string resting in the center of the bow.

- Grab the left side of the spindle with your right hand and the right side of the spindle with your left hand, then twist the spindle clockwise while pulling up slightly to twist the string with the spindle.

You can release your hold on the bow if desired; just make sure the spindle stays in place.

- Place your handhold on top of the spindle with the notch on the tip and hold it in place with your left hand.

- Use your right hand to hold the end of the bow, then start drilling into the hearth board slowly by moving the bow back and forth with pressure as you build up your speed and push down harder. Once smoke begins to emanate, continue drilling until you can't drill any further.

- Remove the spindle and allow it to untwist as it cools down, then grease the tip of the spindle with the oil from your hair or any other source of lubricant. Make sure to only grease the top, which is the side that will be in the handhold.

- Carve a triangular-shaped notch into the socket of your hearth board to form an area for your ember to form. To ensure the ember gets enough air to burn, make sure the triangular-shaped notch is deep enough to almost reach the middle of the hearth board and just shy of the size of ⅛ slice of pie. Also, carve out a little in the bottom to allow for extra oxidation. Then, place a piece of wood or bark underneath the hearth board to catch the ember.

- Repeat the steps for twisting the spindle into the hearth board to begin drilling, but be sure to keep the bow flat and level. You'll also want to maintain a straight arm on the bow and keep your back straight for support. Use the entire bowstring to drill, and apply pressure and increase your speed until you generate enough smoke to form the dust and ember. Fan the ember until it starts to glow, then remove it from the hearth board while sprinkling extra dust onto it to keep the coal burning.

- Put your tinder on the ember and wrap it around it, blowing on it to help grow the flame. Once it bursts into flames, place it on your fire pit.

- Cover the tinder with small pencil-sized sticks at first, and as the flame builds, use larger firewood.

Chemical Combustion

Chemical combustion is the last method for starting a fire in the wilderness that we will be discussing. The most common chemical combustion method is matches. While igniting a fire using a match may appear like a spark method, it is actually chemical combustion that occurs when a match is struck to create a flame. Phosphorous sulfide in a match bursts into flame when heated by friction.

1. Matches.

You can create a one-match fire using the resources available to you:

- Start by setting up your fire pile in the shape of a cone, using twigs, sticks, and kindling (tinder that requires a match to catch fire) to build it up about 1 foot tall. You don't want your pile to lay too close to the ground and you want to pack it in the center with kindling (feel free to go overboard).

- Collect firs, pines, and dead conifer twigs to start your fire with. These contain sticky, highly combustible sap. Combining them with your kindling should be sufficient to get your fire burning with a single match.

- When igniting your fire, you'll want to strike your match as close to your fire pit as possible to limit the distance it has to travel before encountering the fuel. Do your best to shield the match from the wind with your hand and body to ensure it isn't extinguished before starting the tinder/kindling.

- Ignite the fire low in your fire pit to allow it to grow, as fire tends to rise along with heat. Try to light your fire pit in the direction of the wind flow so the breeze will encourage the flames and increase the heat.

2. Battery and steel wool.

Another chemical combustion method is using a 9-volt battery and steel wool. Steel wool is a bundle of flexible, fine, sharp-edged steel filaments that are found in household cleaning products like Brillo pads. The finer the steel wool, the better for your chemical combustion needs.

- Collect a pile of tinder for your fire pit.

- On top of the tinder, place small sticks of kindling.

- Rub the charged end of the 9-volt battery against the steel wool to get an instant spark.

- Steel wool burns very fast, so do this as close to your tinder pile as possible.

- Light the tinder with steel wool to get your fire going and build it up as necessary to keep it burning.

3. Battery and gum wrapper.

If you have a pack or stick of gum with foil or metallic wrapping (i.e. Extra or Wrigley's 5 gum) and an AA battery, you have another option for your chemical combustion fire.

- Collect your tinder into your fire pit.

- Place small sticks of kindling on top of the tinder but allow a lot of space for air.

- Crease the edge of the gum wrapper and tear a long, thin strip.

- Fold the strip in half and cut the edge diagonally.

- Apply each end of the strip to the positive and negative charges of the AA battery to ignite a flame, ensuring the metallic or foil portion of the strip touches the foil side, not the paper side.

- Light your kindling with the flame to get your fire going.

Building Your Fire

Getting your fire started is only one part of the task of getting an ongoing fire burning. You also have to build up your fire to ensure it keeps burning. Many of the steps described above for igniting your fire included preparing your fire pit. Preparing your fire pit and gathering the necessary tinder, kindling, and wood before starting your fire is necessary to ensure you can continue building it.

1.Gathering tinder.

Tinder is any material that is easily ignitable by a spark. Sparking requires dry materials that are small and fine enough to be bundled. Some common, natural resources for tinder include grass, bark, dry leaves, and dry pine needles. Lint and cotton are also great options for tinder. The finer and dryer, the better.

2.Gathering kindling.

As previously discussed, kindling is tinder that requires a match to be ignited. Thus, it also consists of dry and fine materials, but they can be larger than what you'd use for tinder (i.e. small for tinder versus medium for kindling). Twigs, bark, sticks, and dry leaves serve well for kindling.

3.Gathering wood.

Your wood will be the largest of the items needed for your fire. Use it to build your fire and keep it going. Like the other items, it must also be dry as well as dead. Recall that dead wood is seasoned wood that contains little to no moisture (i.e. wood obtained from the underside of deadfalls or dead tree limbs). You'll want to gather wood of various sizes to adequately be able to feed your fire with the appropriate wood size.

Once you've gathered all of your tinder, kindling, and wood for your fire, you're ready to build your fire structure. Since there are multiple options for building your structure, we'll cover three of the most common formations: teepee (also written as tipi), log cabin, and lean-to.

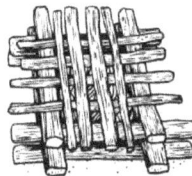

Teepee Formation.

The teepee (or tipi) fire structure is similar to the teepee formation for building your shelter.

- Bundle your tinder into about a 4-inch ball and center it in your fire pit.

- Use your kindling to build a cone around your tinder, stacking it around the tinder. Be careful not to put so much kindling that air can't reach the tinder.

- Lean your logs of wood against the kindling into a teepee formation.

- If you'll be using a lighter or matches to ignite your flame, be sure to leave an opening at the bottom of your teepee to spark the tinder as low as possible. Sparking it low will allow the flames to rise and make a large fire.

- Once you ignite your flame (using the previously discussed methods of starting your fire) and add it to your fire pit, blow and fan the fire as appropriate to spread the flames and grow the fire.

- Once the fire is burning, add wood logs as appropriate in the shape of a teepee to keep your flame going.

Log Cabin Formation.

The log cabin formation can be achieved by creating a small teepee first consisting only of tinder and kindling, then stacking your wood logs around the teepee in an alternating pattern.

- Line the first layer of logs parallel around the teepee, then stack the next row perpendicular, continuing to stack up in an alternating pattern in the shape of a square. The gaps between each layer will enable the air to circulate from the bottom up to the top of your shelter.

- Every 3 layers, make a thin tinder roof with 4 or 5 tinder twigs.

- Once the bed is built, light the kindling in the middle and blow and fan the flame as needed to boost the fire. You can also dig tiny air holes into the ground underneath the first set of legs to increase airflow.

Lean-to Formation.

The lean-to formation is especially handy when you find yourself on windy terrain. It's also a fairly easy fire structure to create.

- Position a large, thick log of wood on the ground next to your tinder, ensuring the log is on the side shielded from the wind (downwind).

- Lean your kindling against the log, angled over the tinder.

- Light the tinder with your flame and add tinder or sticks as necessary to build up your fire.

- Once the fire is roaring, you can add larger logs

Chapter Summary

Knowing how to start a fire can be the difference between life and death in the wilderness. Fire not only provides a crucial source of heat for your body, but it also provides a fuel source to warm liquids to keep your core body temperature warm. If you are stranded for a longer time, you may need a fire to cook food in order to fuel yourself. Being aware of the methods to start a fire is simply a good life skill to have. You're now equipped with a variety of choices to serve your fire-making and building needs.

In this chapter, you learned:

- Various techniques for starting a fire in the wilderness.
- How to prepare to build your fire.
- Different formations of fire beds that you can build in the wilderness.

In the next chapter, you will learn the essentials of finding and purifying water in the wilderness.

CHAPTER 6: WATER

Water is one of the most important natural resources you'll need to survive in the wilderness. Being able to stay hydrated will be crucial to your survival. As previously mentioned in the introduction with the survival Rule of 3s, you can only survive without water for three days. Therefore, next to oxygen and shelter, water will be the most important resource you will find in the wilderness. The human body is around two-thirds water, which is used for internal processes like processing food and circulating blood. Dehydration occurs when your body expels more water than it consumes, which can occur after about six hours without water. Therefore, being able to locate water is an important survival skill.

In normal settings, it is recommended to drink eight 8oz glasses of water per day (known as the 8x8 rule). Being stranded in the wilderness often results in more exertion to survive, so you'll need more than the minimum of two quarts of water in these circumstances. This is not only true for warm or hot environments in which you'll be perspiring more and needing water to replenish your hydration, but also for cold environments. The dry air in cold environments causes your body to lose water through your skin even though you're not perspiring. So, no matter the weather conditions you're facing, you'll need plenty of water to survive the terrain. Luckily, there are plenty of resources available to you in the wilderness that can provide it.

Locating Water Sources

As previously discussed, your shelter should be built near (but not too close) to a water source whenever possible (200 feet away). However, few sources of water are safe for immediate consumption in the wilderness—you may hike up to a clear lake or river and think you've struck gold, but this water can contain millions of organisms (i.e. pathogens, viruses, bacteria, etc.). Depending on the circumstances, drinking water with possible pathogens may be OK if you think a rescue will occur soon. In that case, a hospital will be able to cure any parasites or bacterial infections.

Water flows downhill. Be on the lookout for dips, valleys, and low-lying terrain where water may be flowing. However, avoid any lower elevations you come across (i.e. subalpine areas) because the risk of absorbing harmful pathogens is higher here.

Take note of the vegetation in the area. Any areas with lavish green vegetation are areas where you should be able to find water nearby.

Plants are a water resource. Plants consume water, so they can provide you with a source of water. Strategies for pulling water from plants include consuming the plant itself or extracting the water or sap.

Fruit—For edible sources of water, you can look for fruits such as blackberries or strawberries to readily consume.

Grass—The heavy dew found on grass can also provide readily consumable water:

Tie any absorbent cloth you have available around the shins of your legs, then go for a stroll through the grass before the sun rises to soak up water that can be wrung out for consumption.

Avoid Cacti—While sourcing your water from a cactus may seem like a good option, the pulp is extremely acidic and will lead to diarrhea and/or vomiting if consumed on an empty stomach. This will further dehydrate you and be counterproductive to your survival. Thus, this should not be consumed when depending on water to keep you alive.

Don't forget to use your senses:

- Rest stops along your trail are great opportunities to observe your surroundings.

- Listen for any signs of water flow/streaming. In the wild, it should not be too difficult to hear, especially in an isolated area.

Snow and ice can also be great sources for water in cold weather. Ice has more water supply than snow, so if you have the option, go for ice. However, neither should be consumed in its iced or snow form because ice will cool your core body temperature and increase your risk for dehydration:

- Melt the snow or ice to increase its temperature.

- You'll also want to purify it before consumption whenever possible to reduce the risk of ingesting harmful contaminants.

Most sources will need to be purified before drinking to minimize your risk of illness due to hazardous bacteria or viruses. You should attempt to locate readily-drinkable water first as it will save you time and energy. Your surroundings and the life around the water can indicate where to begin your search for drinkable water.

Animals need water for survival and know where to go to get safe drinking water:

- Observe wildlife and animal activity to see where they go to get their water.

- Take note of any animal tracks/footprints as they may lead you to sources for available drinking water.

- Birds are also a great guide for finding water:

- Their flight paths can direct you toward a water supply.

- Observe their flight paths, both in the morning and evening, to guide you toward drinkable water in the area.

Don't forget about the bugs:

- The presence of certain insects can indicate drinkable water sources.

- Take note of any swarming insects as they typically linger near readily-drinkable water.

Collect Rainwater:

- Rainwater is a safe, bacteria-free water source.

- Capture the water in containers.

- Direct water into a container with a tarp. Tie the edges of the tarp to high points of a tree or bush and use a rock above the container to create the low point where water will naturally flow.

Collect Dew

- Dew is a bacteria-free water source.

- Soak up the water with a cloth and then squeeze the water out into a container.

Condensation

Another method for extracting water is through condensation. Condensation is a great technique to employ in all environments—including the desert. With condensation, you can convert liquid, moisture, and water vapor in the air into drinkable water by using heat (i.e. fire, the sun) and a glass, plastic, or metal object.

Solar Still Condensation Method:

- Locate a moist area that is exposed to sunlight for the majority of the day.

- Dig about 2 inches deep and 3 feet wide in a bowl-shape, as well as a flat sump suitable for your container (i.e. leaf, plastic bag, aluminum can, etc.) in the middle of the bowl. Then, place your container in the middle at the lowest point.

- Cover the hole with plastic, then cover the sides of the holes with soil and rock.

- Put a rock in the middle of the plastic/tarp/canvas above the container that catches the condensation, allowing the plastic/tarp/canvas to sag around 12-inches to shape it into an inverted cone, then pack the edges with soil to further secure it.

- The sun will heat the ground, releasing moisture that then condenses on the plastic cover. The condensation will flow to the lowest point where the rock is and then drip into the container for your water supply.

Bag Around Tree Limb Condensation Method (<u>Transpiration</u>):

- Get a plastic bag and cut a dime-sized hole in the bottom corner of it for water to seep out.

- Locate an easily accessible tree branch that's full of leaves.

- Secure the plastic bag over the branch of leaves with the hole at the bottom, then zip tie it in place.

- Place a container directly under the hole in the bag and allow the water to drip for a day to stock your supply.

Purifying Water

To drink water that is unsafe for immediate consumption, you'll need to purify it. Your options for purification will depend on the resources and environment available to you, but the following options may be applied broadly:

1. Boiling water is both the easiest and best method of water purification when stuck in the wilderness. Boil your water for at least 10 minutes to kill all the organisms to make it safe to drink.

2. Chlorine or iodine purification tablets are a good way to purify water for those who aren't allergic to iodine, so only use them if you're certain you don't have an iodine allergy. If you're dealing with murky water, use more than one tablet to purify the water.

- Allow the tablet to sit in the water for at least half an hour.

- Pour the water in and out of two containers for extra oxidation and improved taste.

3. Solar Water Disinfection (SODIS) is a good option if you have a small (3 liters or less) plastic or glass bottle that is clear and free of scratches:

- If the water you're filtering is murky, filter it through a thin cloth (i.e. bandana) first.

- Place your plastic or glass bottle of water in an area that gets direct sunlight for six to twelve hours.

- Shade decreases the effectiveness, so if it's an area full of cloudy skies, increase the time to two days.

- Once the waiting period is over, the water is ready to drink.

4. UV Purifications. Ultraviolet light concentrated at the correct intensity can generate enough radiation to purify water. There are a plethora of devices available for creating artificial ultraviolet light for purification, but you need to filter the water first to eliminate any larger debris or particles.

5. Filters:

Survival filter straws allow you to consume water through a bacteria-eliminating straw. They can be quite costly, but they are a great resource to have handy to filter water in the wilderness.

Do it yourself (DIY) pinewood filter is another option, but it should be your last resort:

- Wrap a small piece of pinewood tightly with plastic tubing.

- Place a container below one side of the stick of pinewood.

- Pour water onto the other end of the pinewood and the purified water will filter through the pine cork and drip out the other end into your container.

Chapter Summary

Finding a water supply will increase your chances of surviving in the wilderness. Not only do you need to know how to locate a viable source of water, but you also need to be able to distinguish between water sources that may be readily consumed versus sources that will require filtering and purification before drinking. The guidance outlined in this chapter should have enabled you to source out the most optimal methods for obtaining drinkable water while in the wilderness.

In this chapter, you learned:

- How to locate sources for water supply while in the wilderness.
- Different methods for extracting and collecting water in the wilderness.
- How to filter and purify water in the wilderness.

In the next chapter, you will learn about the essential tools needed to survive in the wilderness.

CHAPTER 7: TOOLS

Now it is time to make the tools necessary to survive. Knowing how to craft tools, such as knives, spears, and saws using natural resources will help you to perform all the other tasks needed for your survival. Tools can help cut wood for shelter, slice and notch wood for building your fire bed, and puncture trunks and stems for your water supply. Your ability to identify the proper natural resources to craft your tools can help make every other aspect of surviving in the wilderness easier for you.

Tool Building Blocks

For starters, be on the lookout for animal bones, stones, rocks, and hearty wood. These natural resources will go a long way in creating tools for your survival needs. While we spent a lot of time using wood for shelters, fire, and water when creating tools for your survival, animal bones, stones, and rocks are the best resources. They can be shaped into sharp knives, spears, and saws to serve as tools or weapons to fend off unanticipated predators.

Animal bones can be used to make sharp-edged tools while maintaining flexibility, which makes them a great resource for pointy projectiles, sewing needles, and hook barbs.

Stones and rocks can be hammered with natural resources, chipping off sharp flakes to use for tools. Opt for fine-grained stones for your tool needs; they can be identified by their lack of natural separation lines/planes (pre-defined lines that will cause the stones to split along if hammered, which is not optimal). Your best options will include:

Obsidian—Hard volcanic glass (most commonly located inside lava) that's brittle and can be formed into sharp edges.

Chert—Typically white or black fine-grained rock that sometimes contains small fossils. They come in multiple varieties, including:

Jasper—Glossy rock (similar to obsidian but without the translucence) that is commonly brown, red, green, or yellow.

Flint—Hard, sedimentary rock that sparks when struck against steel. As it will be layered with a cortex (chalk-like coating) when found in the wilderness, you'll need to remove the cortex first so the flint can be exposed for use.

Chalcedony—Silica with extremely fine twines of moganite and quartz, and a waxy luster (found in a variety of colors).

Rhyolite—Volcanic rock that looks similar to granite.

Quartzite—Hard rock, typically found on hilltops and bare ridges.

Felsite/Felstone—Volcanic rock composed of volcanic ash, typically light gray or white, tan, or red.

The first rule to crafting any tool from natural resources in the wilderness is safety. You don't want to expose yourself to danger while locating your resources to create your tools or when hammering and shaping your tools into the proper form. While searching for rocks and stones, you may find yourself on unsteady terrain that can shift with your movements. You will also be dealing with hard and sharp material that can cut and injure you in the actual crafting stage.

Knives

The first tool you'll want to prepare is a knife because you'll likely need this handy tool to help craft all your other weapons and essentials. Two great options for crafting your knife include animal bones and rocks/stone.

1. Animal Bone Knives. If you have access to animal bones, you can hammerstone it into knife-form:

- If you're able to use the bone's natural shape, it will make your job easier. Try to locate flat bones (i.e. leg bones) because they provide great edges when smashed, hammered, and/or sawed into shape.

- Select a hard stone that fits comfortably in your hand to use as a hammerstone, as well as another hard stone to rest the rounded edge of the bone against.

- Begin striking the bone with your hammerstone while moving the bone back and forth as needed, ensuring not to strike against the flat side of the bone because you don't want to break any potential edges needed for your knife. The mission is to crack and break the bone until you break off a sharp edge adequate for your knife's blade.

- Use a sandstone to sand the bone into your desired edge for the blade slowly and carefully. Don't apply too much pressure that will cause the bone to break.

- You can add a handle to the bone by using plant fiber (dry plant fiber from dead plants is optimal):

- To get the fiber off a plant, break the plant stem in half, then pull the fibers off by sliding your thumb and index down the shaft.

- Cord the fiber by gathering the strands of fiber together, twisting from the middle in opposite directions until it folds over on itself, pinching the fold, then twist-braiding the ends around until your cord is completed.

- Align a wooden stick at the other end of the blade for your handle.

- Double over one end of your cord around the stick to create a loop between the stick and the blade, leaving extra cord (long cord end) past the other end of your stick.

- Wrap the short cord end around the stick up toward the loop and tuck it through the loop.

- Pull both the looped short end and long end of the cord to tighten it around the stick to secure it in place for the handle, and scrape the uncorded parts of the stick off with a sharp rock to remove the excess.

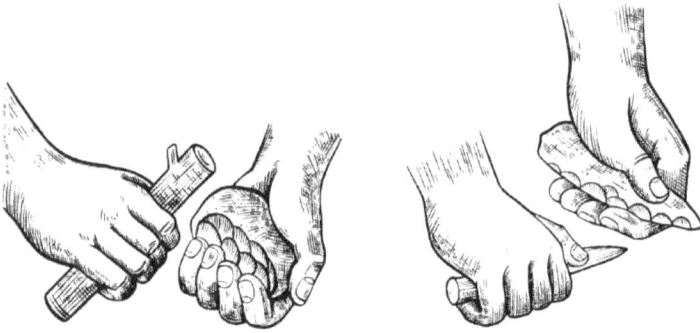

1. Rock Knives. You can make rock knives when you can find quality rocks to shape them with, which is usually in abundance near creeks and hillsides.

- Find a large rock or stone (from the options previously mentioned) that can be used to make your blade.

- Find a hard, medium-sized rock with a rounded surface to use as your hammerstone.

- With the large rock positioned on your thigh, strike the edge of it with the hammerstone in a continuous motion to chip off the edges and yield blades you can use as a knife.

- Use extreme caution when using the rock knife. Cut away from yourself in a slicing motion.

WILDERNESS SURVIVAL ESSENTIALS

Spears & Saws

A spear is another tool that can be made from natural resources, and you can make it either with or without a blade.

1. Bladed Spear. A bladed spear can be made by using the same techniques used to craft your knife blades. The spearhead may be made with either bone or rock as advised above, then connected to the shaft as follows:

- Find a stick around 4-5 feet long and light enough to handle with ease.

- Split the handle of your spear and grove the blade snuggly into the split. Pack any space between the blade and handle with wood and soil.

- Fasten the bladed spearhead to the shaft by wrapping it with plant-fiber cording, in the same fashion described for making a knife handle.

2. Wooden Spear. A wooden spear lacks a blade but is still effective.

- Select a 4-5 foot straight, sturdy wooden stick that you're able to handle with relative ease.

- Place one end of the stick into a flame of fire until a flame appears on the tip to fire-harden it.

- Sharpen the flamed tip with a rough rock until it is sharp enough for use.

Saws

Saws also come in handy in the wilderness. They can be made using hard rocks and pressure flaking. Pressure flaking is the process of applying pressure (instead of striking) to remove narrow flakes along a stone's edge. Pressure flaking a blade of rock will create serrated edges in the rock that can be used as a saw.

Other Tools

There are various other tools you may create in the wilderness besides knives, spears, and saws. As previously mentioned, you can create a cord with plant fiber. That cord won't just be useful for creating your knife handle, but also creating rope. In addition to the natural resources available to make your tools like plant fiber, there are other common objects you may find in the area that you can use as tools:

Flashlights—The flat bottom/surface of a flashlight can be used as a hammer.

Pot—You can create a pot for cooking using wood:

- Locate a healthy piece of wood (i.e. pine, oak, hickory, fir hemlock) suitable in size for the pot size you're aiming for (i.e. big enough to contain 1-2 quarts of liquid after the center has been tunneled out).

- Chip away at one side of the bark until a flat surface is formed.

- Place glowing hot embers from your fire in the center of the flattened surface and blow on them to help them burn through the bark until a bowl shape is formed.

- Scrape out the residue with a sharp stone, then smooth it out with a sanding stone.

Water Bottles—Water bottles aren't only resourceful as fire starters (as previously discussed); you can also use them for fish traps:

- Cut off the neck of the water bottle.

- Invert the neck back inside the water bottle to form a trap for catching small fish.

Inuit Sunglasses—You can create sunglasses to shield your eyes from the sun and/or reflected glare of sunlight from ice/snow/water using plastic, cloth, and/or wood:

- Cut two slits about 5 inches long and ⅛ inch wide into plastic or cloth and tie it around your eyes.

- Cut two slits into wood or bark and use plant fiber to create a cord to secure it on your face.

Chapter Summary

Using natural resources to create tools dates back to the beginning of time. In most cases, this requires creating common tools in their primitive forms. Being able to find the proper materials to make your tools is key. With the options presented in this chapter, you should have little to no problems crafting the tools you'll need to survive in the wilderness.

In this chapter, you learned:

- What natural resources to look for to create tools in the wilderness.
- How to create knives, spears, and saws using natural resources.
- About other tools that can be crafted with materials available in the wilderness.

In the next chapter, you will learn more about creating and using rope in the wilderness.

CHAPTER 8: ROPE

A s briefly discussed in the previous chapter, dead plant fiber is a great resource for cording or making rope. Cording and ropes are not only useful for creating knife handles and fastening your spearheads to their shaft, but they can also be used to help you build shelter, for certain fire-making techniques and for snare lines to catch food, just to name a few functions. The key to creating rope in the wilderness is being able to locate high-quality dead plant fiber.

Fibers for Making Natural Cords

Many fibers can be used to make natural cords in the wilderness. Dogbane is a great option for cording, however, it's poisonous if ingested and may cause adverse reactions due to their latex sap. Thus, if you're allergy-prone or easily-irritable, consider the following options instead:

Milkweed—Less allergenic option than dogbane with soft fiber that can produce cording reminiscent of synthetic string.

Bark—Fallen trees and branches with hanging bark are a great source for strong, coarse fiber. Tulip trees, cedar trees, and white basswood trees offer great sources for tree-based fiber. If using the bark from a cedar tree, choose the fiber inside the bark instead of the strands on the outside of the bark.

Hemp—A very versatile plant that contains highly durable fiber and has a natural resistance to heat from the sun.

Willow Bark—Arguably one of the best options of plant fiber available, they are a great option for strong, durable cordage.

Cattail Leaves—May be used whole and braided into rope or shredded like dead plant fiber and twisted for stronger cordage.

Grass—Stems of grass can be used as-is (without requiring shredding like dead plant fiber). Dunegrass, sweetgrass, and reeds are the best.

Nettle—The stems contain high-quality fiber for cording.

Vines—Vines may be used for light-weight tasks since their fiber isn't as strong as plant fiber.

Creating Your Rope

The type of rope you create may depend on the source of fiber used for cording, but the process of extracting the fiber and cording it into a rope is relatively simple with any source of fiber. The quality of the fiber you use will affect the durability of your rope. When choosing the fiber to extract, aim for brown, tall stalks that are about a year old with high branches.

As outlined in the previous chapter, for dead plant fiber:

1. To get the fiber off a plant, break the plant stem in half, then pull the fibers off by sliding your thumb and index down the shaft.

2. Cord the fiber by gathering the strands of fiber together, twisting from the middle in opposite directions until it folds over on itself, pinching the fold, and then twist-braiding the ends around until your cord is completed. Then, braid your cords together as appropriate to form a rope specific to your needs.

3. For extracting fiber from bark:

4. Break your selected stalks from the lower end where it's brittle enough for easy-breakage by snapping the stalk from side-to-side.

5. Carefully remove any branches from the stalk and the top of the stalk, being mindful to minimize how much fiber you remove in the process.

6. Flatten the stalk against a hard surface to puncture its core, then separate it into halves.

7. Break off about an inch of wood from the thick end of each stalk and remove the wood to produce two ribbons of fiber covered in outer flaky bark.

8. Grind the fiber with your fingers to remove the excess bark.

9. Braid the fibers together to form cords, then braid your cords together as appropriate to form a rope specific to your needs.

Rope Weaving and Braiding Techniques

There are many rope weaving and braiding techniques available depending on the type of rope you're aiming to create for your survival needs:

Solid Braid - A tubular rope formed by intertwining cords of fiber in a circular pattern.

Plaited Ropes:

- Create eight separate cords of fiber and separate them into three piles:

    1. 1 pile of four cords.

    2. 2 separate piles of two cords.

- Intertwine the four-cord pile with the two sections of two-cord piles, with one pair going clockwise and the other going counter-clockwise, alternating until the plaited rope is complete.

Double-Braided Ropes - This type of rope combines two ropes into one by braiding one fully constructed rope over another braid of fully constructed rope (i.e. plaited rope over plaited rope).

Twelve-Strand Braid - For those desiring a hollow, tubular rope, create twelve separate cords from your fiber, then braid each cord over and under each other to complete it.

Hollow and Diamond Braid - A tubular rope that's hollow, formed in a plain-braided pattern.

Knots

After locating cord fiber and learning braiding techniques to construct ropes, you'll also need to learn some common knots. Only the basic knotting techniques are shown below but many people love learning about new knots. Some knots are used for attaching things together while other knots are used to extend the length of a rope. Each technique has its benefits, so be sure to employ the technique that best suits your survival needs.

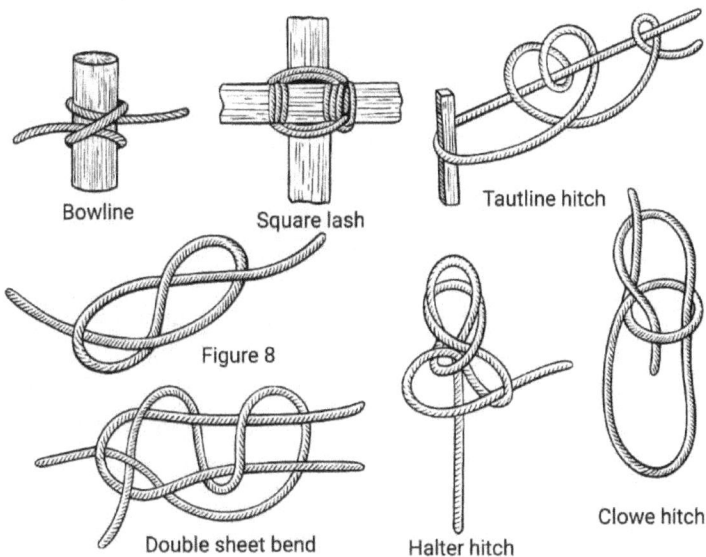

Bowline

Square lash

Tautline hitch

Figure 8

Double sheet bend

Halter hitch

Clowe hitch

1. Figure 8. The Figure 8 is one of the strongest knot formations available, maintaining up to 85% of your rope's strength. This capability makes it an excellent source for hiking and rock-climbing because it allows you to create multiple knots along the entire length of your rope, as well as secure a knot at the end. Although it may be difficult to form for some, it comes in three main variations that provide extra flexibility in its creation:

Basic Figure 8 Knot:

- Create a loop with your rope by crossing one end of your rope over the top of the remaining bit, forming a Q-shape.

- Pinch the top of the loop, then twist it once in the opposite direction of the Q.

- Pull the tail of the Q through the upper loop from behind.

- Pull both ends of the rope to tighten it, forming the classic Figure 8 knot.

Figure 8 Follow-Through Knot allows you to attach your Figure 8 knot to an object securely:

- Create your Q-shape with the rope.

- Pinch the top of the loop, then twist it once in the opposite direction of the Q.

- Pull the tail of the Q through the upper loop from behind, then wrap the end around the object you want to attach.

- Pass the same end of the rope back through each loop, forming a big loop, then around the big loop you've formed.

- Pass the same end of the rope along the upper rope and pull it through the right loop, resulting in both ends being on the opposite side of your attached object.

- Pull both ends of the rope to tighten it and complete the follow-through.

Figure 8 on a Bight Knot allows you to attach your rope to a climbing harness or carabiner:

- Fold your rope in half, then create your Q-shape.

- Pull the ends of the Q through the loop.

- Pull both ends of the rope to tighten it and secure your loop to be attached to your harness or carabiner.

2. Bowline. The bowline knot is an alternative to the Figure 8 and is typically used in rescue scenarios. It's a self-tightening rope that allows you to secure the rope around a person, and it's also a great option for hanging food:

- Create your desired size loop with your rope with the loose end stretching from right to left across the standing portion of the rope.

- Use your right hand to grip the standing end of the rope, then twist it clockwise downwards for half a turn to force the other end to poke through the small loop.

- Pass the standing ends through the loop again and tighten the rope as needed.

3. Clove Hitch. This is another method for connecting a rope to the desired object that allows you to adjust the length of the rope without untying the knot. The clove hitch is a great technique that can also be applied for anchoring. It offers you the flexibility of adjusting your knots in an easier way than other techniques, but it tends to loosen after constant movement:

- Loop your rope around the object you want to connect it to, crossing the looped end over the remaining rope.

- Make a counter-clockwise loop around your object, passing the end of the rope through the newly formed loop.

- Pull both ends of the rope to tighten the knot around your object.

3. Double Sheet Bend. A sheet bend knot connects two pieces of rope together. Since a single sheet bend knot isn't the most secure knot you can form, the double sheet bend makes it more secure, giving extra durability to your combined ropes. It's great for combining ropes with various dimensions together more securely:

- Create a half-loop with the thicker of the two ropes.

- Slide one end of the thinner rope underneath the loop and around, then around the thick rope.

- Repeat the above step to double the knot.

- Grip the thick rope with one hand while pulling the two ends of the thinner rope with your other hand to tighten it.

4. Taut Line Hitch. This is a knotting technique that allows you to attach your rope to an object and glide it up and down the object to the desired position for tightening and/or loosening:

- Loop your rope around your desired object for attachment.

- Wrap the loose end of the rope around the loop twice along the inside of the loop.

- Lay the loose end of the rope over the double-loop, then wrap it around the straight rope, pulling the loose end through the newly formed loop to create an adjustable knot.

5. Halter Hitch. A resourceful knotting technique, which is another option for anchoring as it allows you to connect your rope to an object while also being able to swiftly release its grip by pulling one end of the rope:

- Loop your rope around your desired object for hitching.

- Pull the working end of the rope under and through the loop.

- Cross the working end to create another loop, then tuck that loop under your first loop.

- Fold the working end of the rope through the small loop to lock it into place.

- Pull on the loose end of the rope to tighten it around your object as necessary.

- Adjust your hold around the object by pulling the knot to your desired position and pulling the ends to tighten it.

6. Square Lash. A great knotting technique to employ for cross braces when you need to secure two objects into place until you're able to tie or bolt them down:

- Cross your two objects together at a right angle.

- Connect a rope to the vertically-lying object with a clove hitch (as instructed above).

- Pull the loose end of your rope under the horizontally lying object on the left side.

- Wrap the loose end of the rope in front of the vertical object, then over the horizontal object.

- Repeat the step above twice.

- Next, repeat the fastening process by wrapping the rope around the front and back of the vertical object.

- Once completed, your rope should be lashed into a square-shape that can be tied off with a half hitch.

Chapter Summary

Having a rope in the wilderness can be essential to your survival. They can be used to help you with building your shelter and crafting vital tools to help you survive while in the wilderness. Knowing how to locate the proper fibers in the wilderness to construct your rope is the first step you need to take. Not all knots are created equally and should not be used universally, therefore, be sure to apply the appropriate roping and knotting techniques given in this chapter to alleviate your survival abilities and ensure maximum safety.

In this chapter, you learned:

- How to find viable, natural resources to create a rope in the wilderness.
- Multiple braiding techniques to create ropes specific to your survival.
- Various knotting techniques to serve your survival needs in the wilderness.

In the next chapter, you will learn how to signal for help in the wilderness.

CHAPTER 9: SIGNALING FOR HELP

t's time to get you out of the wilderness by signaling for help. While distress signaling seems to be underrated in comparison to some of the other wilderness survival essentials, it's just as vital. As with all other survival essentials, your signaling options will be dependent on what is available to you. Distress signals come in various forms, and while modern technology has made many of us reliant on using our cell phones to contact emergency responders, if you're stranded in the wilderness, the likely presumption is that you don't have cell phone access. Even if you happen to have a cell phone handy, you may be in an area with no reception. If you can, hike as high as you can to increase the chances of getting reception. However, this section assumes you don't have that as an option and therefore focuses on ways to signal for help.

Mirror

A mirror can save your life when you're stranded in the wilderness. Out of all of the distress signals available, a signal mirror is one of the best ways to get the attention of searchers. When searchers are looking for you, a momentary glint of light can catch their attention and lead them to investigate further. Mirrors with sighting lenses work best, but if your mirror doesn't have a sighting lens, it can still be effective when used properly. And, if you don't have a signal mirror at all, you can make one by using any of the following:

- A standard mirror (i.e. makeup mirror or hand mirror).
- Flat objects with aluminum foil wrapping (i.e. Hershey's Chocolate Bar wrapping paper).
- Objects that have reflective surfaces (i.e. glasses).
- A survival blanket folded.

To send a distress signal with your mirror:

- Hold your mirror under your eye with one hand.

- Extend your other hand with your palm up, facing a target in the distance (i.e. hilltop, helicopter, person, etc.).

- Use your thumb and index finger to form a V-shape with your target centered in the "V".

- Angle the mirror to direct the beam of sunlight at the base of your "V", then angle it up to your target.

- Pan the mirror extremely slow from left to right and up and down to send your distress signal. The flashes of light will attract attention.

Smoke and Fire

Fire isn't only essential for keeping you warm and heating your water and food, it can also be used to signal for help. Fire not only produces heat, but it also produces smoke that rises and/or causes light in dark areas. Thus, fire and smoke serve as one of the most identifiable distress signals available when stuck in the wilderness. They're not only effective at night but during the day too, since certain emergency responders (i.e. rescue helicopters, planes, and crew, etc.) have undergone specialized training to identify fire and smoke signals while attempting rescue operations.

When building a fire for a distress signal, one fire won't be enough—you'll need to make three separate fires about 100 feet apart in a triangular fashion. The **three-fire triangle** is an international signal for rescue, meaning that it is one of the most recognizable distress signals you can send, no matter where you are around the world. You can also form the three fires in a straight line about 100 feet apart as an alternative, but the triangle formation is your best option if you have the space to create it. The key is to make all three fires if possible, especially if you're sending your signal during daylight because the thickness of the combined smoke will be more visible than the smoke a single fire would create.

To send your distress signal with fire:

- Go to an open area where your smoke and fire will be visible.

- Make sure the area is contained enough so the fire doesn't spread, such as in the middle of dry grasslands during high winds.

- To build your fire for maximum effect during the day and produce a lot of smoke, the flame has to be big and strong enough to burn items that aren't typically easy to burn. For signal fires during the day, you want to fuel your fire with plastic, rubber, green logs and sticks, and damp, rotten wood.

You'll also want to avoid building your fire under trees or a forest canopy because the smoke will dissipate as it travels through the vegetation and won't be as thick—which defeats the purpose.

- To build your fire for maximum effect at night, you'll want to make it as bright as possible. Therefore, you'll want to fuel it with items that burn easily, like the items you'd normally use to build your campfire (i.e. dry wood).

Whistles and Audible Signals

Sound is another great tool to use as a distress signal. Searchers are trained to recognize the universal audible distress signal of **three whistles**. Blasting three whistles can alert anyone within earshot that you need help. A **humble whistle** is a whistle designed for distress signals, but any whistle will do. If you have the option, select whistles in bright colors for easier spotting and whistle using an attachment (i.e. ring, clip, lanyard, etc.) to minimize the risk of it getting lost.

For cold terrains, you'll want a pealess whistle with no moving parts. Any saliva passed through the whistle can freeze the cork balls found in pea whistles, preventing its movement and disabling the whistle. When using whistles to send distress signals, be sure to remain in your location until help arrives, so your rescuer(s) can follow the sound back to you.

If you don't have a whistle with you, you can use your mouth and/or fingers. Using your mouth alone to whistle may produce a lower pitch than optimal. For a high-pitched whistle, whistle loudly with your fingers in your mouth.

To whistle with your fingers:

- Curl your fingers into your palms except for the index fingers which should be extended and touching together. Your index fingers are making a triangle.

- Open your mouth and tighten your lips against your teeth.

- Place your fingers in your mouth and push your tongue to the back of your mouth. Your incisors should rest on the inside of your first knuckle.

- Your lips should be tight around your fingers and the only way for the air to escape is through the small gap between your fingers and your lips.

- Blow air forcefully through the gap between your fingers and your lips.

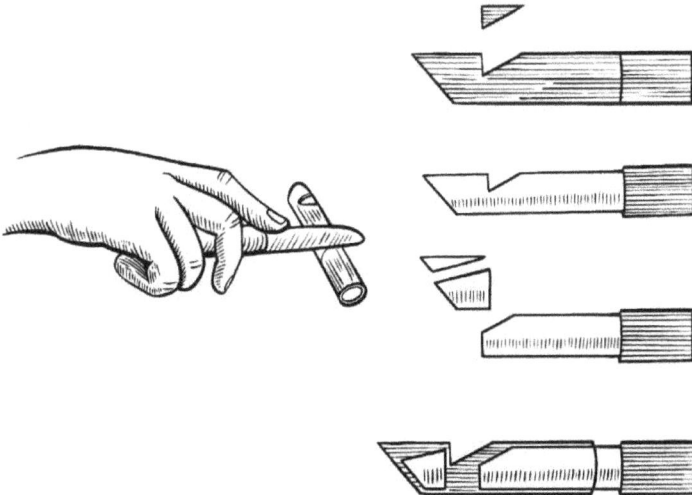

You can also make a whistle using the natural resources available to you:

- Locate a hollow object, such as a bamboo stick, hollow bone, knotweed, reed, or branch of pithy wood.

- Reduce your selected object to between 6-10 inches long and under 1 inch in diameter. The skinnier the better, as you'll be able to blast higher and sharper whistles with a slimmer whistle. For optimal effectiveness, close off one end.

- Cut a slit about ¼ inch deep around an inch from the top of the open end.

- Go to the center of the body and cut from the center back to the first slit near the opening, which should form a shape similar to a "U" but with a sharp bottom.

For your mouthpiece:

- Locate a piece of soft wood (such as willow) on a stick that can fit snugly into the body of your whistle and cut off about 1 inch.

- Cut off about ⅛ of an inch from the end of the stick you will use to blow into when whistling, narrowing it down to around 1/16 removed from the end that will be inserted into the body of your whistle.

Slide your stick into the body of the whistle and attempt to blow:

- If there is sound, your whistle is ready to use.

- If there's no sound, adjust the stick until you're able to hear a sound or shave off a little more of the stick until it produces sound.

There are also other ways you can send audible signals outside of whistles. For instance, you can create a makeshift drum with hollow hardwood, sticks, and rocks. If you can locate a hollow log of hardwood, prop it up on some rocks and beat it with some hardwood sticks (aim for the sticks that make the loudest noise against the drum). The rocks under the log will also help reflect the vibrations for optimal signaling.

Ground-to-Air Signals

Rocks and sticks aren't only great for audible signaling as in a drum, but they can also be used to send a visual distress signal to searchers overhead with ground-to-air signals. Ground-to-air signals are a great option for sending distress signals on islands or in areas with thick woods since emergency responders will likely be airborne. With a ground-to-air signal, you can use rocks, sticks, logs, and even the sand or dirt of the terrain to form messages for help.

Start by locating a large open area. Gather any large rocks, boulders, logs, tree branches, and extra clothing around that contain colors contrasting with the surrounding area. The fact that these colors are different helps it stand out to searchers. For example, if the terrain is bright green, use dark logs and rocks to contrast; if the terrain is white or dark, use bright colors like green leaves and pines. The starker the contrast, the better the chance of your message being seen.

Form the letters for your message using the items you've gathered, and make sure your message spans about a yard wide and a few yards tall. You want your message to be big enough to be read clearly from the air. Some common choices to send as air distress signal messages include:

- "HELP" is a universally known ground-to-air distress signal known to emergency responders worldwide for signaling for help when stuck in the wilderness.

- "SOS" is also a universally known distress signal for wilderness emergency responders.

- "X" is a commonly recognizable signal for conveying the need for medical assistance.

- "V" is a less known signal that conveys you're requesting help.

You'll also need to be aware of possible responses you may receive from airborne emergency responders in planes:

- If the responders circle around your message, it is likely they don't understand what it means. You need to make it more visible to them, so they better understand your request. They may be trying to check your status as well. Also, raise and lower both arms to catch their attention so they don't mistake it for an old signal.

- If the responders reply by tilting the wings of the plane back and forth, your message has been received and help is on the way.

- No matter which response you receive, once your ground-to-air message has been seen by emergency responders, light a fire to further confirm your location.

Flashlights

Flashlights are another resourceful tool to signal for help at night and in heavily shaded areas. This is true for both standard and cell phone flashlights if you have either one with you. When using your flashlight for distress signaling, it's important to preserve the battery for as long as possible, so you'll need to quit using it for any other purpose other than flashing distress signals.

Sending distress signals with flashlights requires utilizing a consistent pattern, such as three consecutive flashes at a time between prescribed intervals. To send a more commonly known distress signal using your flashlight, you can transmit SOS signals in Morse code as follows:

- Three fast flashes of light. (• • •) is Morse code for S
- Three long flashes of light. (— — —) is Morse code for O
- Three fast flashes of light. (• • •)
- Pause, then repeat as necessary until help arrives.

Flags

Using flags is another primitive option for sending a distress signal that's been used for thousands of years. They can easily be created using both natural and non-natural resources available to you:

- You can use any bright clothing and/or gear that can contrast against the surrounding terrain to create a flag by tying the garment to a stick.

- If you have a poncho or tarp that isn't being used, you can create a large flag by tying it to a large stick or tent pole.

- Large, reflective materials like space blankets also make great flags.

Once you've created your flag, you have the option of waving it back and forth to send your distress signal, tying it as high up as possible to a tree or other standing structure, or laying it out on the ground of an open and visible area for ground-to-air signaling.

Flare Signals

Flare signals are also universal beacons used to send distress signals. Flares discharge a bright light to signal for help. They can be handheld or come in the form of flare guns.

1. Handheld Flares. Handheld flares are used as visual distress signals that you would wave in the air to signal for help. If needed, you can attach the flare to a long stick or pole with duct tape or cording to make it taller. However, you'll want to refrain from waving the flare directly overhead in the event it unexpectedly comes loose and falls on you. You'll also want to be mindful of making sure the flare doesn't burn down to your stick or pole or start an unintended fire.

2. Flare Guns. Flare guns are great options when handy. They shoot flares into the air to send distress signals to emergency responders. When using a flare gun, be aware of the possible danger that may be caused to the area when the flare makes contact with the surrounding terrain. To avoid possible wildfires, refrain from using flare guns in dry areas like barren grasslands or bushy areas and pine forests. For safety precautions, it's highly recommended that you limit your use of flare guns to areas with open water like wetlands.

Survey Tape and Sharpies

Survey tape and sharpie markers can also help you send distress signals in the wilderness. Vibrant survey tape (i.e. electric pink or blue) can be used as flags or to mark your trail for emergency responders to follow you, pinpoint existing trails, and leave messages. Add a sharpie marker to the mix and you can add clear messages on the survey tape for responders to read.

Sharpie markers can also be used if you don't have survey tape. You can use them to mark practically any dry surface in the area with messaging for emergency responders, and you can also use them to place markers on your trail as breadcrumbs to find your way back when exploring.

What to Do When Airborne Help Arrives

You also need to know what to do when help arrives to ensure they can reach you as fast as possible, especially if your emergency responders are airborne. As previously advised, airborne emergency responders will likely acknowledge being able to see your signal by responding via circling the message if they don't understand, or tilting the wings back and forth if they read you loud and clear. They may also signify acknowledgment of your messaging by flying low, flashing their lights your way, or dropping down a message of their own to you.

For a swift rescue, assist your airborne emergency responder(s) by preparing the area for landing. Remove all loose materials that may get sucked into the aircraft's rotors or propellers. If you're in an area where the aircraft can't touch down directly near you, navigate towards the landing and signal with noise and any safe visual signals (i.e. flags, mirrors, flashlights, etc.) so they can identify where you are. No matter the circumstances, be sure to adhere to any instructions given by your emergency responders carefully and swiftly.

Chapter Summary

Being able to signal for help can be the difference between being stranded in the wilderness indefinitely and getting the help you desperately need in the nick of time. Considering the extreme conditions, you must know the best distress signaling options available to you based on the resources at your disposal, should you find yourself needing them.

In this chapter, you learned:

- Why knowing how to signal for help is vital to your survival in the wilderness.
- Various methods of sending distress signals.
- What to do when emergency responders arrive.

In the next chapter, you will learn about finding food in the wilderness.

CHAPTER 10: FOOD

As the survival Rule of 3s indicates, you're capable of surviving up to three weeks in the wilderness without food. That's why, despite how much your stomach may crave food while stranded in the wilderness, it's the last of the essentials you need to be concerned with.

Being able to build shelter, locate readily drinkable water, purify other sources for water, and build a fire to keep you warm will all help you survive the wilderness while you wait for help to arrive. Sending distress signals will help you get the attention of emergency responders as fast as possible, so you can be rescued. Your ability to find food is less pressing because it doesn't reach fatal levels unless you've been unable to find food after being stranded for three weeks. However, once all other essentials have been sufficiently addressed, you can start foraging for food.

Not every seemingly edible source of food you may come across is safe for consumption. There are many poisonous and hazardous items out there, so the last thing you want to do is ingest anything that may be harmful to you. As a general rule of thumb when sourcing food for survival in the wilderness, if you are unsure of what something is, don't eat it, especially when it comes to vegetation. Another rule of thumb is to stay away from all things bright in the wilderness. In the wilderness, bugs, plants, marine life, and amphibians with bright colors are more likely to kill you, so avoid them at all costs. Luckily, there are many other food options available to you in the wilderness.

Insects and Bugs

Another general rule of thumb for sourcing food is that, despite how unappetizing they may seem, most insects are not only usually safe to eat but are also a great source of protein. The key is knowing how to distinguish between what is safe versus what you should avoid. Insects are a great source of fuel when out in the wild. In comparison to a usual protein source like beef, which contains about 20% protein, insects provide anywhere between 65-80% protein. Keep in mind that, although most insects are safe to eat, other bugs are <u>not</u>. So, when dealing with creepy crawlers, remember:

Insects can generally be defined as six-legged bugs with a three-part body, an exoskeleton, a pair of antennae, and sometimes wings. Some insects that you may usually be able to consume safely include:

Grasshoppers and crickets—High in protein and found in many areas; just make sure to avoid any bright-colored hoppers because they may be poisonous.

- Grasshoppers are best to catch in the early morning hours because they move slower.

- Crickets are more typically found in damp, dark places like under logs, rocks, and other large objects.

- Check for them in shrubs, trees, and tall grasses. You can also shake tree branches.

- You can catch grasshoppers and crickets by hand; placing a wool blanket or flannel shirt in an area they're known to be (they will get caught on the fibers of the fabric, allowing you to pluck them off); or burying the cut-off top of a plastic water bottle into the ground and shining light over it to attract them into the trap.

Ants—Ants are just about everywhere, extremely simple to catch, and are actually quite tasty.

- You can eat ants raw—just ensure they're dead so they don't bite you in the process.

- You can also catch an entire army of them by locating their home/anthill, hitting their habitat with a stick a few times, and inserting the stick into the opening to collect ants on it. To neutralize their acidity, dunk the stick into a container of water to boil for about six minutes before eating them.

Termites—This is another great source of protein that spends the majority of its existence buried in wood and away from harmful parasites. To locate them, simply split open a cold log of wood, shake them out into a frying dish, and put them over a fire.

Worms—These bugs can be found in abundance and are safe to eat in the wilderness. You can locate them crawling around on the ground after a rain shower or dig them up from under damp soil. Before consuming them, clean them in a water bath for a few minutes to allow them to be cleansed naturally before eating.

<u>**Avoid all insects with bright colors, adult insects that bite or sting, hairy insects like spiders, caterpillars, flies, mosquitoes, ticks, and insects with pungent odors.**</u>

Plants

As previously advised, you should avoid eating any plants you cannot positively identify because it may be deadly. However, considering the variety of vegetation you may encounter in the wilderness and the possibility of mistaking deadly plants as safe, the following guidelines may be applied:

- Refrain from consuming **mushrooms**. Despite some varieties of mushrooms being safe, many are extremely toxic and deadly. When trying to survive in the wilderness, mushrooms are not worth the risk when there are plenty of other viable options available.

- Steer clear of plants with **thorns** or **white** or **yellow berries**.

- Avoid any vegetation with **shiny leaves**, **leaves with groups of threes**, or plans that contain **umbrella-shaped flowers**.

- Any plants or beans that contain **seeds inside a pod** should not be eaten.

- Plants that emanate an **almond smell** should not be consumed.

- Any vegetation with **milky** or **discolored sap** should be avoided at all costs.

- If you do happen to bite into any plant that has a **soapy** or **bitter taste** to it, spit it out immediately.

- Outside of the above plants to avoid, you can use a universally known edibility test on any other plant you encounter to gauge whether or not it's safe to eat:

- Take a strong sniff of the plant to see if it smells rotten or otherwise repugnant. If so, don't eat it.

- Rub the plant against your skin and/or lips for about three minutes.

- If you don't have a physical reaction to the plant (i.e. burning, itching, tingling, etc.), you can begin to assume it's safe to consume and give it a small bite.

- Hold the plant in your mouth to see if you have a reaction and gauge its taste. If there's no soapy or bitter taste and you don't have a physical reaction to the plant, you can eat a little more of it and wait a few hours to ensure you don't have any adverse reactions. If you are still completely fine, you can assume it's safe to eat in larger commodities.

Now that you're aware of plants to avoid and how to subject unknown plants to an edibility test before ingesting, here are some plants you can safely consume while in the wilderness:

Grass—Most grasses are non-toxic and can be consumed raw.

Dandelions—Not only good for making a wish, but dandelions can also be eaten raw or boiled in water, as well as drunk as a tea with boiled water.

Clovers—Easy to chew and can be consumed raw or after boiling in water.

Cattail—Plants typically found in wetlands with a rootstock that can be consumed raw or after boiling in water.

Burdock—Mostly prominent in the eastern hemisphere, they can be large and do contain many edible parts from the leaves to the stalk (after being peeled).

Chicory—Another plant that may be eaten raw or boiled in water.

Pennycress—A commonly found plant worldwide that can be consumed if needed, but should be consumed with caution after assuring the area it's growing in isn't contaminated with hazardous minerals. And any patches growing on the side of a road should never be eaten.

Tree nuts—A fattier and calorie-dense option that's also packed with protein and offers a multitude of edible varieties:

- Hickory nuts
- Be sure not to confuse them for buckeye because it is poisonous.
- Acorns from oak trees:
- Requires preparation
- Crack the shell with a rock to extract the nuts.
- Soak in water to remove tannic acid and bitter taste.
- Pine nuts from pine cones.

Animals and Game

When considering animals as a wilderness food source, you need to know the distinction between regular animals and large game. Game is considered any animal that is typically hunted either for its meat or sport. Although all game are animals, not all animals are considered game. For your wilderness survival purposes, try to catch smaller animals first because they will be more abundant than larger game, are easier for you to catch, and easier for you to prepare. The key to catching them is knowing their habits and behavioral patterns. You can use the following habits and patterns for targeting animals as your food source:

- Animals with seemingly fixed feeding areas.

- Animals with trails spanning from one area into another.

- Animals that live collectively in a certain area in dens or nests.

- Most animals that walk, crawl, swim, or fly.

1.Animals.

Turtles - Great source for fatty meat, which is preferred over consuming solely lean meat (i.e. rabbit) because having too much of the latter may lead to diarrhea.

- Avoid the claws and jaws, even after killing.
- Boil the entire turtle so that the back shell is softened.
- Remove the back shell.
- Cut the undershell into quarters and simmer all of the cut quarters.
- Remove the undershell before eating the meat.

Porcupines - Packed with nourishment and fatty meat.

- Use a rock or stick and give it a swift blow to the head to kill.
- Be sure to avoid any contact with the quills.
- Remove the quills by skinning the porcupine from the underbelly.

Snakes and scorpions - Although they may be intimidating, they're great food sources in the wilderness once they've been safeguarded:

Cut off the snake's head and/or the scorpion's stingers to remove the venomous portion, then either bury or burn the head and/or stingers to keep them from being consumed by other food foragers.

Snakes - Remove the skin and the entrails, then cook. You can also use the bladder of a snake to hold any liquids (i.e. water), so it can serve a dual purpose as both a container and food.

Scorpions - May either be eaten raw or cooked. Avoid the extremely small ones because their poison tends to be deadlier than the larger ones.

2. Game animals. When pursuing game, it's important to note that different areas have different prohibitions on what game you can and cannot hunt, so avoid any illegal game. An animal that has been running will result in meat with a bitter taste because of the lactic acid produced by the activity.

Rabbits - Should be eaten sparingly as they will only provide lean meat.

- They rely more on camouflage than flight for defense.

- Don't show signs that you are eyeing it when approaching it.

Squirrels - Excellent food source that is commonly found in several areas. Throw a rock or stick at it to disable it or use a snare to catch it.

Small Birds/Quail - They don't travel far, so they can be easily pursued with a trench and corral that will prevent them from taking flight.

Eggs - Bird eggs are a good option, but beware of being dive-bombed by a nest protector. Also, be sure to leave some eggs behind so you won't eliminate future generations.

When hunting animals and game in the wilderness, it's important to be aware of the energy you are exerting to catch and prepare it. If there are easier options available that will conserve your energy such as snares and traps, or if you expect emergency responders to arrive soon, hunting animals and game may not be worth the energy. If you do pursue this food source, it's recommended to cook it before eating it to kill off any parasites that may be inside the animals. Cooking your food also allows it to be digested with less energy.

To cook your animal/game (the following cooking instructions may also apply to fish):

1. Skin the animal.

2. Clean out any guts.

3. Clean your hands thoroughly before proceeding.

4. Roasting your meat (or fish):

   • Use a green stick as a skewer and line it with the meat you want to roast.

   • Seal the juices first by holding the skewer of meat directly into the fire briefly.

   • Roast the skewer above the flames of the fire to cook.

   • You can also wrap your meat around a stick or even sandwich your meat between a split stick. Split the stick open and insert some meat to roast it. Prop the stick up on branches that allow it to sit over the fire for roasting.

5. Grilling your meat (or fish):

   • Form a cooking slab using green hardwood or a flat rock (never use rocks that were found in water because the heat may cause the water inside to expand and explode).

   • For animals with backbones, they may be removed first to enable it to lay flatter on the slab.

   • Peg your animal or fish to it and put the slab directly over the coals to grill it.

6. Boiling your meat (or fish):

- Find a rock with a cavity big enough to fit your water and meat.
- Build your fire around the rock cavity to preheat it and add water to boil your meat (or fish).

7. Barbeque your meat (or fish):

- Allow your campfire to burn all the way down to hot coals.
- Lay rows of green sticks across the coals to form your grill.
- Put your meat on a stick (i.e. skewer) and allow it to slow cook over the coals.

Fish and Seafood

Fish is an excellent food source that may provide balanced nutrition while in the wilderness, making it one of the best options available to you. Low tides near the ocean or large lakes allow you to catch edible food (i.e. marine snails clinging to rocks) that you can scoop up with your hands and eat without cooking. There are even more options available to you if you can use your available resources to create fish hooks, fishing poles, and/or nets.

1. Crustaceans. These are your freshwater options that usually form colonies, including some common shellfish like shrimp, crayfish/crawfish, and crabs.

- **Shrimp** - Look for them in highlighted spots at night, anywhere between the shore's edge to about ten meters deep into the water. Scoop them up with a net.

WILDERNESS SURVIVAL ESSENTIALS

- **Crabs** - You can also look for these in highlighted spots at night anywhere between the shore's edge to about ten meters deep into the water. Use bait to attract them and catch them with a net or trap.

- **Crayfish** - More active at night but may also be found during the day under and around stones set in streams. They can even be located in the soft mud of their nests, identifiable by chimney-like holes for breathing.

2. Mollusks. These include some other common freshwater options like mussels, clams, and snails that may be caught using a trap or net. It is best to cook these.

- Look for mollusks in shallow areas with muddy or sandy bottoms, in freshwater or on rocks, and in tidal pools along the shore.

- **Snails** - Often found closer to water, clinging to rocks and seaweed.

- **Mussels** - Usually found in dense colonies located at the base of boulders, inside pools of rocks, and on logs.

3. Fish. Great source of fat and protein.

- To catch them, you'll need to monitor their habits.

- They are attracted to light at night.

- Typically rest near rocks or eddy areas instead of in heavy currents.

117 | P a g e

- May also be found in and around logs and submerged foliage, under areas with overhanging bushes, and in deep pooled areas.

- Should always be cooked to kill parasites.

To catch fish in the wild, you'll likely need to prepare fishing tools and collect bait to attract the fish:

Pot trap—Great for catching small fish:

- Locate a plastic bottle.

- Cut the top of the bottle off.

- Poke a few holes in the bottom of the bottle.

- Put a few small rocks in the bottle.

- Take the cut-off top and invert it inside of the open bottle, sliding it all the way down to the bottom as snugly as possible.

- Tie a fishing line (i.e. dry plant fiber) to the bottom of the bottle for a handle.

- Tie the other end of the string to a sturdy base, such as a tree branch.

- Insert some sort of bait. This can be a worm that you dig up or a grasshopper, etc.

- Place your trap in the water and let it catch your fish.

Bait—Berries, worms, grasshoppers, and insects can serve as bait, so use whichever options you have available to you that you're not currently relying on for sustenance.

Fishing line—Dead plant fiber may be used for your fishing line.

Fishing pole/rod:

- Find a long stick or light log and remove any branches or leaves.

- Test the strength of your rod by bending it to see if it snaps (any portion that does snap off will strengthen your pole after being removed).

- Use cordage to tie a knot at the end of the stick to serve as a handle for grip.

- Tie your fish line (i.e. dead plant fiber) around the center of the stick, then wrap it around a few times.

- Tie the end of your fishing line around the tip of your pole and add your hook (if not already attached).

Fish hook options—You can make a fish "gorge" hook using thorns, animal bones, or wood:

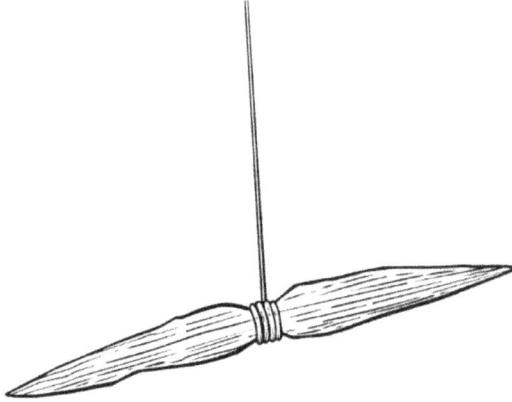

Simple hooks - Less effective, but easily made:

- Locate a small stick and remove the bark.

- Sharpen each side of the stick into points.

- Tie your fish line (i.e. dead plant fiber) to the middle of the stick, then your hook will be complete.

Thorn hooks - Only use for small fish.

- Collect sharp thorns from tree branches or sticks.

- Prepare a long, thin piece of cordage.

- Stick the thorn through the eye at the end of your cordage.

- Wrap the remaining cordage around the stem of the hook, then pass the end of your cordage underneath the last wraps of cordage and pull it tight to finish off your hook.

Wishbone hooks:

- Snap off half of one of the wishbone legs from an animal (i.e. bird, chicken, etc.).

- Using the short end of the leg bone, sharpen an edge of the bone to create a sharp point. Be careful not to break it.

- Just under the point you created, carve a barb to complete your hook.

- At the other end of your newly-made hook, poke a hole through it to attach your fishing line to.

Wood hooks:

- Find a stick about the size of your index finger.

- Break off a third of the stick and strip the bark off it.

- Sharpen the broken third of the stick into a point.

- Tie the sharpened point the remaining ⅔ of the stick with your fishing line (i.e. dead plant fiber) to create a V-shape.

Chapter Summary

As you can see, many food sources are available to you when stuck in the wilderness. Knowing which sources are safe to eat and how to obtain them is key. Knowing which sources can be readily eaten versus sources requiring preparation and cooking is also vital to your survival. You never want any survival essential to work against you, so ingesting harmful parasites, bacteria, or viruses should be avoided. With the variety of food sources available and your newfound knowledge on which foods to avoid, your ability to locate a range of food sources in the wilderness should be less daunting and relieve some worries about what you should or should not eat while stuck in the wild.

In this chapter, you learned:

- Foods to avoid when stuck in the wilderness.
- Various vegetation, insects, animal, game, and fish that may be used as food sources in the wilderness.
- How to trap, catch, prepare, and cook plants, animal, game, and fish with the natural resources you can find.

CONCLUSION

Being able to survive in the wilderness isn't something we naturally learn from our parents, in school, or on the job. It's not something that many people even consider unless they are preparing for an outdoor adventure or expecting to be in wilderness areas where they know they'll need to deploy skills specific to their survival. Sadly, outside of survivalists, a lot of people who find themselves stranded in the wilderness don't have functional cell phones handy to call for help, let alone prepackaged items like BOBs, sleeping bags, tents, or tarps to help them survive the elements. Therefore, knowing primitive survival methods in the wilderness becomes crucial. The wilderness survival essentials outlined in this book can be an amazing aid for equipping yourself to survive any extreme condition using the natural resources available to you. It can now serve as your guide to surviving the wilderness until help arrives.

Navigating the unknown is stressful enough, so preparing yourself by becoming more informed about what to expect and how to survive will allow you to remain as calm as possible in the wilderness, which is not only essential for preserving the energy you need to survive but also crucial to minimizing your risk of encountering dangerous elements such as predators that can sense your fear or angst. The Survival Rule of 3s is a great place to start when prioritizing your needs essential to your survival.

So, unless you have a photographic memory or an innate ability to retain every essential addressed in this book, recall that on average a human can live:

- 3 minutes without oxygen/air or immersed in icy water.
- 3 hours in harsh terrains without shelter (this includes clothing).
- 3 days without water if they are sheltered from harsh terrains.
- 3 weeks without food if they do have shelter and water.

Knowing how long you have to obtain your essentials allows you to address each essential appropriately, and understanding how to use the resources available to you to facilitate your survival needs is paramount to being able to properly gather, prepare, and/or build your essentials within the timeframe necessary. When out in the wilderness, being aware of the survival essentials provided to you in this book will enable you to more readily prioritize your needs and know how best to serve them while waiting for help to arrive.

As a final tool to aid you in your wilderness survival, the following are a few more tips to assist you with navigating the wilderness, so you can avoid getting lost and wasting valuable time and energy while trying to survive the elements

Compass—You can make a compass if you don't have one handy:

- Get a container of water (i.e. large leaf that can hold water).

- Locate a needle (i.e. paperclip, razor blade, sewing needle, etc.) that can be magnetized (may be done by rubbing the needle against a magnet about thirty times).

- You can also magnetize a needle by rubbing it from the needle's eye to it's point about 100 times on animal hair, wool, silk or your hair. The trick is to always move in the same direction lifting up between strokes (not back and forth).

- Float the magnetized needle on another smaller leaf while it's in water, then wait for it to orient from North to South.

Sun/Shadow Orienting—If you don't have a compass, you can use the sun and shadows to help you navigate:

- Locate a straight stick, plant it into the ground to stand up straight, and use the tip of its shadow to represent <u>West</u>.

- Let about twenty minutes pass, then mark the tip of the shadow again.

- Connect your second mark to the <u>West</u> mark to denote <u>East</u> to <u>West</u>.

- Stand with the <u>West</u> mark to your left and the <u>East</u> mark to your right. The direction you are facing is <u>North</u>. The opposite direction (behind you) is <u>South</u>.

- Moss can also indicate which direction is <u>North</u> when the skies are cloudy since they typically grow more prolifically on the North end of trees and slopes.

- Spiders can also indicate which direction is <u>South</u> in warm weather, as they generally tend to spin their webs on the south side of trees.

Walking Downstream—Water flows downstream, and populations tend to be at lower elevations. If you follow the stream downwards, you should be heading toward civilization.

Now that you have all of the essentials necessary for you to survive in the wilderness, you can better prepare yourself for the unknown. Practice the tools and guidance provided to you in this book before your next outdoor adventure so you will be more familiar with executing them. As with most—if not all—skills, practice makes perfect.

Being able to test out any tool you may need before you actually have to use it in a survival situation will make it smoother when you really do need it. Besides, where's the fun in learning how to survive if you never get to use the skills you've obtained? In any case, if you do find yourself needing to depend on these wilderness survival essentials, remain calm, refer to the Survival Rule of 3s, and deploy everything you've learned in this book to survive until help arrives.

What Did You Think of Wilderness Survival Essentials: Handbook for Finding Shelter, Water and Food?

First of all, thank you for purchasing this book **Wilderness Survival Essentials***. I know you could have picked any number of books to read, but you picked this book and for that I am extremely grateful.*

I hope that it added at value and quality to your everyday life. If so, it would be really nice if you could share this book with your friends and family by posting to Facebook *and* Twitter.

If you enjoyed this book and found some benefit in reading this, I'd like to hear from you and hope that you could take some time to post a review on Amazon. Your feedback and support will help this author to greatly improve his writing craft for future projects and make this book even better.

I want you, the reader, to know that your review is very important and so, if you'd like to **leave a review***, all you have to do is follow the link below:*

You can follow this link to https://www.amazon.com/gp/customer-reviews/write-a-review.html?asin=B0871WFTYH *now.*

I wish you all the best in your future adventures!

Thank you!

Rolf